The
GOVERNMENT OF GOD

The
GOVERNMENT OF GOD

By
JOHN TAYLOR,
One of the Twelve Apostles of the Church of Jesus Christ
of Latter-day Saints.

"O let the nations be glad and sing for joy: for thou shalt judge the people righteously, and govern the nations upon earth."—Psalm lxvii.

This publication retains the original spelling, punctuation, and content of the source material. Any errors or inconsistencies are preserved as they appeared in the original text.

ISBN: 979-8-89368-012-6

A 2025 reprint of the 1852 edition.

Compiled, printed and bound in the U.S.A.

For more information, visit www.TruthBoundPublishing.com.

Republished by

Table of Contents

Preface iii

Chapter I.

The Wisdom, Order, and Harmony of the Government of God. ..1

Chapter II.

The Government of Man 8

Chapter III.

On the Incompetency of the Means Made Use of by Man to Regenerate the World. 18

Chapter IV.

What Is Man? What Is His Destiny and Relationship to God? 33

Chapter V.

The Object of Man's Existence on the Earth; and His Relationship Thereto 39

Chapter VI.

Man's Accountability to God... 57

Chapter VII.

The Lord's Course in the Moral Government of the World 66

Chapter VIII.

Whose Right Is It to Govern the World? Who Has Governed It?.70

Chapter IX.

Will Man Always Be Permitted to Usurp Authority Over Men, and Over the Works of God? Will the World Remain For Ever Under a Curse, and God's Designs Be Frustrated? 83

Chapter X.

Will God's Kingdom Be a Literal or a Spiritual Kingdom? 101

Chapter XI.

The Establishment of the Kingdom of God Upon the Earth 108

Chapter XII.

The Effects of the Establishment of Christ's Kingdom, or the Reign of God Upon the Earth... 128

Preface

It was Elder Taylor's intention to superintend the publishing of *The Government of God* in person, previous to his departure for Great Salt Lake City last spring; but the numerous cares attending the French and German Missions, of which he was President; the translation of the Book of Mormon into the French and German languages; the establishment of *L'Etoile du Déseret* at Paris, and *Zions Panier* at Hamburg; together with a multitude of other business connected with the welfare of the Kingdom of God, rendered it impossible.

The manuscript was therefore handed to me by Elder Taylor, with a request to superintend the printing of the work, which I have done to the best of my ability.

Considering the disadvantages arising from the Author's absence during the reading of the proofs, I believe it is as correctly rendered, as was possible from a manuscript copy.

The Work is now before the Public, and from one portion at least it will meet with a cordial reception, treating as it does upon the theme most dear to their hearts—the Reign of Righteousness and Peace.

From other portions it will meet with varied reception, but will nevertheless lead the minds of all to contemplate the glory of that time when the Messiah, even Jesus, shall come with all his holy angels, and sit upon the throne of his glory, and govern all nations upon earth.

James Linforth.
Liverpool, August, 1852.

Chapter I.

The Wisdom, Order, and Harmony of the Government of God.

The Kingdom of God is the government of God, on the earth, or in the heavens. The earth, and all the planetary systems, are governed by the Lord; they are upheld by his power, and are sustained, directed, and controlled by his will. We are told, that "by him were all things created that are in heaven, and that are in earth, visible and invisible, whether they be thrones, or dominions, or principalities, or powers; all things were created by him, and for him: and he is before all things, and by him all things consist."[1] Collos. i. 16, 17. If all things, visible and invisible, are made by and for him, he governs and sustains all worlds to us known, together with the earth on which we live. If he governs them, they are under his dominion, subject to his laws, and controlled by his will and power.

---

[1] I wish here to be understood, that at present I am writing to believers in the Bible. I may hereafter give my reasons for this faith; at the present I refer to the Scriptures without this.

If the planets move beautifully, and harmoniously in their several spheres, that beauty and harmony are the result of the intelligence and wisdom that exist in his mind. If on this earth we have day and night, summer and winter, seed time and harvest, with the various changes of the seasons; this regularity, beauty, order, and harmony, are the effects of the wisdom of God.

There are two kinds of rule on the earth; one with which man has nothing directly to do, another in which he is intimately concerned. The first of these applies to the works of God alone, and His government and control of those works; the second, to the moral government, wherein man is made an agent. There is a very striking difference between the two, and the comparison is certainly not creditable to man; and however he may feel disposed to vaunt himself of his intelligence, when he reflects he will feel like Job did when he said, (xlii. 6.) "I abhor myself, and repent in dust and ashes."

In God's government there is perfect order, harmony, beauty, magnificence, and grandeur; in the government of man, confusion, disorder, instability, misery, discord, and death. In the first, the most consummate wisdom and power are manifested; in the second, ignorance, imbecility, and weakness. The first displays the comprehension, light, glory, beneficence, and intelligence of God; the second, the folly, littleness, darkness, and incompetency of man. The contemplation of the first elevates the mind, expands the capacity, produces grateful reflections, and fills the mind with wonder, admiration, and enlivening hopes; the contemplation of the second produces doubt, distrust, and uncertainty, and fills the mind with gloomy apprehensions. In a word, the one is the work of God, and the other that of man.

In order to present the subject in a clear light, I shall briefly point out some of the leading features of the two governments.

The first, then, is that over which God has the sole control, such as the heavens and the earth, for "He governs in the heavens above, and in the earth beneath." It may be well here to say a few words on His moral government, in the heavens. All we can learn of that is very imperfectly set forth in the Scriptures. It would seem, however, that all was perfect order, for "He spake, and said, Let there be light, and there was light; and He divided the light from the darkness." "He spake, and the waters were gathered together, and the dry land appeared." And in the creation of the fish, the fowls, the beasts, the creeping things, and man, it was done in the councils of God. The word was, Let us do this, and it was done. It would seem, then, that that government is perfect in its operations, for all the mandates of God are carried out with the greatest exactitude and perfection. God spake, chaos heard, and the world was formed.

We find also that transgression is punished; when Satan rebelled he was cast out of heaven, and with him those who sinned.

Here, then, in these things consummate wisdom was manifested, and power to carry it out.

The plan of redemption was also made thousands of years ago. Jesus is spoken of by the prophets as being "The Lamb slain from before the creation of the world." The future destiny of this earth is also spoken of by prophecy; the binding of Satan; the destruction, and redemption of the world; its celestial destiny; its becoming as a sea of glass; the descent of the new Jerusalem from heaven; the destruction of iniquity by a power exercised in the heavens, associated with one on the earth; and a time is spoken of where John says—"Every creature which is in heaven, and on the earth, and under the earth, and such as are in the sea, and all that are in them, heard I saying, Blessing, and honor, and glory, and power, be unto Him that sitteth upon the throne, and unto the Lamb for ever and ever." Rev. v. 13. But I shall let this pass for the present, and content myself with saying on this subject, that in the councils of God, in the eternal world, all these things were understood: for if He gave prophets wisdom to testify of these things, they obtained their knowledge from Him, and He could not impart what He did not know; but "known unto God are all his works, from the beginning of the world." Acts xv. 18. God, then, has a moral government in the heavens, and it is the development of that government that is manifested in the works of creation; as Paul says, "The invisible things of Him from the creation of the world are clearly seen, being understood by the things that are made, even his eternal power and Godhead." Romans i. 20.

But when we speak of the heavens, we mean also the planetary system; for the world, and other worlds are governed by principles independent of man. The power that causes this earth to roll on its axis, and regulates the planets in their diurnal and annual motions, is beyond man's control. Their revolutions and spheres are fixed by nature's God, and they are so beautifully arranged, and nicely balanced, that an astronomer can calculate the return of a planet scores of years beforehand, with the greatest precision and accuracy. And who can contemplate, without admiration, those stupendous worlds, rolling through the immensity of space at such an amazing velocity, moving regularly in their given spheres without coming into collision, and reflect that they have done so for thousands of years. Our earth has its day and night, summer and winter, and seed time and harvest. Well may the poet say that they—

"Proclaim for ever, as they shine,

The hand that made us is divine."

And here let me remark how different is this to the works of man. We see, then, the power of God manifested in their preservation and guidance; but when we reflect a little further, that while our planetary system rolls in perfect order round the sun, there are other systems which perform their revolutions round their suns; and the whole of these, our system with its centre, and other systems with their centres, roll round another grand centre: and the whole of those, and innumerable others, equally as great, stupendous, and magnificent, roll round another more great, glorious, and resplendent, till numbers, magnificence, and glory, drown the thought, we are led to exclaim with the prophet, "O the depth of the riches both of the wisdom and knowledge of God! how unsearchable are His judgments , and His ways past finding out!" Romans xi. 33. Without referring again to the motions of our earth, and the beautiful regularity and precision of the whole of this elegant machinery, we will turn our attention a little to the works of creation as found on the earth. The make, construction, and adaptation of each for its proper sphere, are the work of God; and they are all controlled by His wisdom and power, independent of man. In the conformation of the birds, the beasts, the fishes, the reptiles, the grains, herbs, plants, and trees, we see a striking exemplification of this fact. No matter which way we turn our attention, the same order and intelligence are displayed. The fish in their organization are peculiarly adapted to their proper element; the birds and beasts to theirs; the amphibious animals to theirs. The nicely organized machinery of their bodies; their bones, muscles, skins, feathers, scales, or hair; the formation of their bodies, their manner of living, together with the nature of their food, and their particular adaptation to the various elements and climates which they occupy, are all so many marked evidences of skill, forethought, intelligence and power. We will here notice a few examples. Plunge bird, beast, or man, into the water, and let them remain there, and they will soon die; take a fish out of the water, and death ensues; yet all are happy, and move with perfect enjoyment in their proper spheres. Elevate a man, beast, or fish, into the air, and let them fall, and they will be bruised to death; but the bird, with its wings, light bones, and fragile body, is peculiarly adapted to the aerial element in which it moves, and is perfectly at home; while the brute creation and men feel as much so on the earth. Again, their habits, food, coatings, or coverings, digestive powers, and the organization of their systems, are all peculiarly adapted to their several situations. The same principle is developed in their arrangement and position on the earth. Those that inhabit a southern climate are peculiarly adapted to that situation; while those that inhabit a northern are equally fitted for theirs.

Take the reindeer and polar bear to the torrid zone, and they would be out of their proper latitude, and would probably die. Remove the elephant, lion, or tiger, to Iceland or Greenland, and leave them to their own resources, and they would inevitably perish.

We will notice for a moment the construction of their systems. Each one is possessed with muscular strength, or agility, according to its position, wants, or dangers, and there is a beauty, a symmetry, and a perfection about all God's works, which baffle and defy human intelligence to copy. An artist is considered talented if he can make, after years of toil, a striking likeness of any of those things, either on canvas, or in marble. But when he has done, it is only a dead outline; remove a little paint, or tear the canvas, and its beauty is destroyed; break the arm of a statue, and we see nothing but a mutilated stone. But take a man, for example, and remove the skin, there is still order and beauty; remove the flesh, there is still workmanship and skill, and the bones, the flesh, the muscles, the arteries and veins, and the nerves, and the lungs, not to forget the exquisite fineness of the sensitive organs, manifesting a skill, a forethought, a wisdom, and a power, as much above that of man as the heavens are above the earth.

We see the power, wisdom, and government of God, displayed in the amazing strength of some of the largest of the brute creation; as also in the fineness and delicacy, of the arrangement of the smaller. And while we admire the stupendous power of the elephant, we are equally struck with the fineness, delicacy, and beauty of some of the smaller insects. The prescience, and intelligence of God, are as much manifested in arranging the bones, muscles, arteries, and digestive organs of the smallest animaculæ, as in the construction of the horse, rhinoceros, elephant, or whale. I might touch upon the organization of plants, herbs, trees, and fruits; their various compositions, modes of nourishment, manner of propagating their kind, &c.; but enough has already been said upon this subject. It is one that no one will dispute upon; Jew and Gentile, black and white, Christian and Heathen, philosopher and fool, all have one faith on this subject.

I have briefly touched upon it for the purpose of presenting in a clear light the imbecility and weakness of man; for wherever we turn our attention, we see power, wisdom, prescience, order, forethought, beauty, grandeur and magnificence.

These are the works of God, and shew His skill, workmanship, glory, and intelligence. They reflect His divine power, and shew in unmistakeable characters the wisdom of his government, and the order that prevails in that part of creation over which He has the sole and unlimited control.

We can perceive very clearly that what God has done, is rightly done. It is not governed by instability and disorder, but continues from eternity to eternity to bear the impress of Jehovah.

Chapter II.

The Government of Man.

We will now turn our attention a little to the government of man, and see how that will compare with the foregoing, for man stands at the head of this beautiful creation; he is endued with intelligence and capacity for improvement; he is placed as a moral agent, and has the materials put into his hands to work with, the works of his Father as a pattern, the conduct of many of the inferior creation as an example—and might make the earth a garden, a paradise, a place of uninterrupted happiness and felicity, a heaven below. And if God had not delegated this moral agency and power to man, and thus given him the privilege, in part, of being the arbiter of his own destiny, such it would have been to this day, like the Eden from which he was ejected because of his transgression. For he had everything placed within his power, and was made lord of the creation. The beasts, birds, fish, and fowl, were placed under his control; the earth yielded plenty for his wants, and abounded in fruits, grain, herbs, flowers and trees, both to satisfy his hunger, and to please the sight, taste, and smell. The fields waved with plenty, and produced a perennial harvest. The fruits teemed forth in all their luscious varieties to satisfy his most capacious desires.

The flowers, in all their gaiety, beauty, and richness, delighted the eye; while their rich fragrance filled the air with odoriferous perfumes. The feathered tribes, with all their gorgeous plumage and variety of song, both pleased the eye, and enchanted and charmed the ear. The horse, the cow, and other animals, were there to promote his happiness, supply his wants, and make him comfortable and happy. All were under his control, to contribute to his happiness and comfort, supply his most extended desires, and to add to his enjoyment; but with all these privileges what is his situation?

With celestial blessings within his reach, he has plunged down to the very verge of hell, and is found in a state of poverty, confusion, and distress. He found the earth an Eden —a paradise; he has filled it with misery and woe, and has made it comparatively a howling wilderness. And let us not blame Adam alone for this state of things; for after his ejection from Paradise, the earth was sufficiently fertile to satisfy all the desires of man with moderate industry, and is at the present day, if it were not for the confusion that exists, and if men were properly situated, and its resources developd. But more of this anon.

At present we will examine some of these evils, and then point out their cause, and the remedy. We find the world split up and divided into different nations, having different interests, and different objects; with their religious and political views as dissimilar as light and darkness, all the time jealous of each other, and watching each other as so many thieves; and that man at the present day (and it has been the case for ages), is considered the greatest statesman, who, with legislation or diplomacy, can make the most advantageous arrangement with, or coerce by circumstances, other nations into measures that would be for the benefit of the nation with which he is associated. No matter how injurious it might be to the nation or nations concerned, the measure that would yield his nation an advantage, might plunge another in irremediable misery, while there is no one to act as father and parent of the whole, and God is lost sight of. What is it that the private ambition of man has not done to satisfy his craving desires for the acquisition of territory and wealth, and what is falsely called *honor* and *fame*?

Those private, jarring interests have kept the world in one continual ferment and commotion from the commencement until the present time; and the history of the world is a history of the rise and fall of nations—of wars, commotions, and bloodshed—of nations depopulated, and cities laid waste. Carnage, destruction, and death, have stalked through the earth, exhibiting their horrible forms in all their cadaverous shapes, as though they were the only rightful possessors. Deadly jealousy, fiendish hate, mortal combat, and dying groans, have filled the earth, and our bulwarks, our chronicles, our histories, all bear testimony to this; and even our most splendid paintings, engravings, and statuary, are living memorials of bloodshed, carnage, and destruction. Instead of men being honoured who have sought to promote the happiness, peace, and wellbeing of the human family, and greatness concentrating in that, those have been generally esteemed the most who produced the most misery and distress, and were wholesale robbers, ravagers, and murderers.

And from whence come these things? Let the apostle James answer: "From whence come wars and fightings among you? Come they not hence, even of your lusts that war in your members? Ye lust, and have not—ye kill, and desire to have, and cannot obtain: ye fight and war, yet ye have not, because ye ask not. Ye ask, and receive not, because ye ask amiss, that ye may consume it upon your lusts." James iv. 1-3. Here is evidently a lack of that consummate wisdom, that moral and physical control, that parental power which balances the universe, and directs the various planets. For let the same recklessness, selfishness, individuality, and nationality there be manifested, and we should see the wildest confusion.

Man has come in contact with man, morally, physically, religiously, and nationally, from the foundation of the earth. If God's works had done so, what tumult and ruin there would have been in the immensity of space! Instead of the order that now prevails, man would have been sometimes frozen to death, and at other times burned up; one or two seasons of irregularity, even in climate, would depopulate the earth. But what if the planets, irrespective of the power by which they are controlled, were to rush wildly through space, and, with their mighty impetus dash against each other? "What fearful consequences would ensue." There would be "system on system wrecked, and world on world." What terrible destruction and ruin! We have read of earthquakes destroying countries, of wars depopulating nations—of volcanoes overwhelming cities, and of empires in ruin; but what would the yawning earthquake, the bellowing volcano, the clang of arms, or a nation's distress, be in comparison to a scene like this? System would be shattered with system; planet madly rush on planet; worlds, with their inhabitants, would be destroyed, and creations crumble into ruins. There would be truly a war of planets, "a wreck of matter and a crash of worlds." These, indeed, would be fearful results, and shew plainly the distinction between the beautiful order of God's work, and the confusion and disorder of man's. God's work is perfect—man's imperfect. The one is the government of God, and the other that of man.

We notice the same mismanagement in the arrangement of cities and nations. We have large cities containing immense numbers of human beings, pent up, as it were in one great prison-house, inhaling a fœtid, unwholesome atmosphere, impregnated with a thousand deadly poisons; millions of whom, in damp cellars, lonely garrets, and pent up corners, drag out a miserable existence, and their wan faces, haggard countenances, and looks tell but too plainly the tale of their misery and wretchedness. A degenerate, sickly, puny race tread in their steps, inheriting their fathers' misery and distress.

If we notice the situation of the nations of Europe at the present time, we see the land burthened with an overplus population, and groaning beneath its inhabitants, while the greatest industry, perseverance, economy, and care, do not suffice to provide for the craving wants of nature. And so fearfully does this prevail in many parts, that parents are afraid to fulfil the first great law of God, "Be fruitful and multiply, and replenish the earth;" and by desperate circumstances are almost forced to the unnatural wish of not propagating their species; while, corrupted with a correspondent depravity with that which reigns among nations, they are found using suicidal measures to prevent an otherwise numerous progeny from increasing their father's misery, and inheriting his misfortunes. And yet, while this is the case, there are immense districts of rich soil, covering millions of square miles, inhabited only by a few untutored savages, or the wild beast of the forest; and such is the infatuation of man that in many districts of country, which were once the seats of the most powerful empires, and where flourished the mightiest nations, there is nothing but desolation and wildness. Such are Nineveh and Babylon, on the Asiatic Continent; and Otolum, and many others discovered by Stephens and Catherwood, in Central America; and recently discovered ruins—unequalled in the old world—a little above the head of the California Gulf. Not only their cities, but their lands are desolate, deserted, and forsaken, and the same evils that once existed there are transferred to another soil, all bespeaking plainly that we want a great, governing, ruling principle to regulate the affairs of the world, and assist poor, feeble, erring humanity.

THE GOVERNMENT OF GOD

Again, if we examine some of the details of these evils, we shall see more clearly the importance and necessity of a change. Nearly one-third, speaking in general terms, of the inhabitants of the earth are engaged in a calling that would be entirely useless if the world were set right.

If men and nations, instead of being governed by their unruly passions, covetous desires, and ambitious motives, were governed by the pure principles of philanthropy, virtue, purity, justice, and honor, and were under the guidance of a fatherly and intelligent head, directed by that wisdom which governs the universe, and regulates the motions of the planetary systems, there would be no need of so many armies, navies, and police regulations, which are now necessary for the protection of those several nations from the aggressions of each other, and internal factions. Let any one examine the position of Europe alone, and he will find this statement abundantly verified. Look at the armies and navies of France and England; and the confusion of Germany, also of Austria, Turkey, Russia and Spain, not to mention many of the smaller nations, and let their armies, their navies, and police be gathered together, and what an abundant host of persons there would be. They would be sufficient to make one of the largest nations in the world! And what are they doing? To use the mildest term, watching each other, as a person would watch a thief for fear of being imposed upon, and robbed, or killed; but generally strolling around as the world's banditti, robbing, plundering, and committing aggressions upon each other; and if they have peace, acquiring it by the sword; and if prevented from aggression and war, it is generally, not that they are governed by just, or virtuous principles, but because they are afraid that aggression might lead to combinations against them which would result in their overthrow and ruin.

In the city of Paris alone, at the present time, and its immediate environs, there are one hundred thousand soldiers, besides police to a very great number, not to mention the vast number of custom-house officers and others. Suppose we add to these their families, where they have any, and where they have not, notice the vast amount of prostitution, misery, degradation, and infamy, that such an unnatural state of things produces. I give the above as an example of the whole, but here the navies are not included. I say again, What are these all doing? They do not raise corn to supply the wants of men, nor are they occupied in any useful avocation; but they *must* live, and their wants must be supplied by the products of the labour of others. There has to be an immense amount of legislation for the accomplishment of this thing, and instead of having one government of righteousness and the world obeying, we have scores of governments, all having to be sustained in regal pomp, to be equal to their neighbouring nations; and all this magnificence and national pride having to be supported by the labour of the people. Again, all these legislatures have to provide immense hosts of men, in the shape of custom-house, excise, and police officers, to carry out their designs, all of whom, and their families, help to increase the burden, till it becomes insupportable. That, together with the unnatural state of society, before referred to, in regard to the situation of the inhabitants of cities and the nations, plunges millions of the human family into a state of hopeless destitution, misery, and ruin, for they are groaning under all these hopeless burdens without having sufficient land to till to meet their demands, and as natural means fail they are obliged to have recourse to those that are unnatural. Hence, in England a great majority of the inhabitants are made slaves of, virtually to supply the wants of the greatest part of the world, and are forced to be their labourers. Thousands of them are immured in immense factories, little less than prisons, groaning under a wearisome, sickening, unhealthy labour; deprived of free, wholesome air; weak and emaciated, not having a sufficiency of the necessaries of life.

Thousands more from morning till night are immured in pits, shut out from the light of day, the carol of the birds, and the beauty of nature, sickly and weak, in many instances for want of food; and yet, in the midst of their wretchedness, gloom, and misery, you will sometimes hear them trying to sing in their dungeons and prison-houses, in broken, dying accents, "Britons never shall be slaves."

I will here give, as one example, an iron works that I visited lately in Wales. One of the proprietors informed me that they employed fifteen thousand persons, and paid them £5,000 per week. Most of these people laboured under ground, in the pits, digging for iron ore and coal; the remainder were employed principally about the furnaces, in rolling the iron, &c., at heavy, laborious, fatiguing work. And who were they toiling for? Principally for the Americans and Russians, at that time, to furnish them with railroad iron. And what did they get for their labour? The riches of those countries? No. £5,000 a week among about fifteen thousand persons. I suppose, however, a number of these were boys and girls. The average wages of men was from ten to twelve shillings per week. And this is their pay for that labour; and yet the masters are not to be blamed, that I can learn, for they are forced by competition to this state of things, and by the unnatural, artificial state of society. If they did not do this their workmen must be out of employ, and ten times worse off, if that were possible, than they are now. In the State of Pennsylvania, in America, where the railroads run through coal and iron mines both, they leave them untouched, and come to England for iron to make the rails of, that they cannot afford to make at home, because of higher wages, and an *outlet* to society, which prevents them from being coerced into bondage. If the world was right, the labour would be done there, and not here, and the labour of carriage saved.

The situation of the peasantry and workmen in France, Germany, Prussia, Austria, and Russia, and in fact I may say of Europe generally, is worse even than that of the same class in England; and wherever we turn our attention, we see nothing but poverty, distress, misery, and confusion; for if men do not copy after the good and virtuous, they generally do after the evil. When nations and rulers set the pattern, they generally find plenty to follow their example; hence covetousness, fraud, rapine, bloodshed, and murder, prevail to an alarming extent. If a nation is covetous, an individual thinks he may be also; if a nation commits a fraud, it sanctions his acts in a small way; and if a nation engages in wholesale robbery, an individual does not see the impropriety of doing it in retail; if a strong nation oppresses a weak one, he does not see why he may not have the same privilege; corruption follows corruption, and fraud treads on the heels of fraud, and all those noble, honourable, virtuous, principles that ought to govern men are lost sight of, and chicanery and deception ride rampant through the world. The welfare, happiness, exaltation, and glory of man, are sacrificed at the shrine of ambition, pride, covetousness and lasciviousness. By these means nations are overthrown, kingdoms destroyed, communities broken up, families rendered miserable, and individuals ruined. I might enter into a detail of the crimes, abominations, lusts, and corruptions that exist in many of our large cities, but I shall leave this subject, and conclude with the remarks of the prophet Isaiah, who gazed in prophetic vision on this scene: "Behold, the Lord maketh the earth empty, and maketh it waste, and turneth it upside down, and scattereth abroad the inhabitants thereof... The earth also is defiled under the inhabitants thereof, because they have transgressed the laws, changed the ordinances, and broken the everlasting covenant. Therefore hath the curse devoured the earth, and they that dwell therein are desolate." Isaiah xxiv. 1, 5 and 6.

Iniquity of every description goes hand in hand; vice, in all its sickening and disgusting forms, revels in the palace, in the city, in the cottage; depravity, corruption, debauchery, and abominations abound, and man, that once stood proudly erect in the image of his Maker, pure, virtuous, holy, and noble, is vitiated, weak, immoral, and degraded; and the earth, which was once a garden, not only brings forth briars and thorns, but is actually "defiled under the inhabitants thereof."

Those great national evils of which I have spoken are things which at present seem to be out of the reach of human agency, legislation, or control. They are diseases that have been generating for centuries; that have entered into the vitals of all institutions, religious and political; that have prostrated the powers and energies of all bodies politic, and left the world to groan under them, for they are evils that exist in church and state, at home and abroad; among Jew and Gentile, Christian, Pagan, and Mahomedan; king, prince, courtier, and peasant; like the deadly simoon, they have paralyzed the energies, broken the spirits, damped the enterprize, corrupted the morals, and crushed the hopes of the world.

Thousands of men would desire to do good, if they only knew how; but they see not the foundation and extent of the evil, and long-established opinions, customs and doctrines, blind their eyes, and damp their energies. And if a few should see the evil, and try a remedy, what are a few in opposition to the views, power, influence, and corruption of the world?

No power on this side of heaven can correct the evil. It is a world that is degenerated, and it requires a God to put it right.

Chapter III.

On the Incompetency of the Means Made Use of by Man to Regenerate the World.

I purpose in this Chapter to shew the incompetency of the means made use of by man for the accomplishment of the purposes of God—the establishment of His Kingdom, or Millennial reign.

Now, if it is the kingdom of God, that is to be established, it must be introduced by God. He must not only be the originator of it, but the controller also, and any means short of these must fail of the object designed.

The great evils that now exist in the world are the consequences of man's departure from God. This has introduced this degeneracy and imbecility, and nothing but a retracing of his steps, and a return to God can bring about a restitution.

God gave to man a moral agency, as head of the world, under himself. Man has usurped the sole authority, and taken upon himself to reign and rule without God. The natural consequence is, that we have inherited all the evils of which I have spoken, and nothing but the wisdom, goodness, power, and compassion of God, can deliver us therefrom, restore the earth to its pristine excellence, and put man again in possession of those blessings which he has forfeited by his transgression. Emperors, kings, princes, potentates, statesmen, philosophers, and churches, have tried for ages to bring this state of things about; but they have all signally failed, not having derived their wisdom from the proper source. And all human means made use of at the present time to ameliorate the condition of the world must fail, as all human means have always done.

There are some who suppose that the influence of Christianity, as it is now preached and administered, will bring about a Millennial reign of peace. We will briefly examine the subject.

First, we will take the Greek and Catholic Churches as they have existed for ages—without an examination of their doctrines, whether right or wrong—for they form two of the largest branches of the Christian Church. They have, more or less, governed a great portion of Europe at different times; and what is the situation of the people and nations where they have held sway? We have noticed the effects, and already briefly touched upon the evils that prevail in those countries; and if Greece and Russia, or any other country where the Greek Church has held sway, be a fair specimen of the influence of that church, we have very little prospect, if that religion were more widely diffused or extended, that the results would be more beneficial, for if it has failed in a few nations to ameliorate their condition, it would necessarily fail to benefit the earth if extended over it. Nor do we turn with any better prospect to the Catholic religion. Of what benefit has it been to nations where it has prevailed the most? Has there been less war, less animosity, less butchery, less evil of any kind under its empire? It cannot be said that it has been crippled in its progress or its operations. It has held full sway in Spain, Rome, and a great portion of Italy, in France and Mexico for generations, not to mention many smaller states.

Has it augmented the happiness of those nations of the world? I need not here refer to the history of the Waldenses, and Albigenses, and Huguenots, to that of the Crusades, wherein so many Christian kings engaged; nor to the unhappy differences, the wars and commotions, the bloodshed and carnage, that have existed among these people, for their history is well known. And the present position of both the Greek and Roman churches, presents a spectacle that is anything but encouraging to lead us to hope, that if the world were under their influence, a Millennial reign of peace and righteousness would ensue.

And let not any one say that these churches have not had a fair opportunity to develop themselves, for their religion prevailed and was cherished in those nations. They have held universal sway, at different times, for generations. The kings, councils and legislatures, have been Catholic or Greek. In Rome, the Pope has ruled supreme, and also for some time in Lombardy, Ravenna, and other States. In Greece, the Patriarch of Constantinople, and in Russia, the Emperor, is head of the church.

But, methinks I hear the Protestants say, we fully accord with you thus far, but we have placed Christianity on another footing. Let us examine this subject for a moment.

The question would naturally follow, What have the reformations of Calvin, Luther, and other reformers, done for the world? We may notice that Denmark, Sweden, Prussia, with a great part of Germany, Holland, and Switzerland, as also England and the United States, are Protestant. What can we say of them? That they are a part of the disorganized world, and have manifested the same unhappy dispositions as other portions. Reform has not altered their dispositions or circumstances. We see among them the same ambitious, grasping, reckless disposition manifested, and consequently the same wars, bloodshed, poverty, misery, and distress; and millions of human beings have been sacrificed to their pride, ambition, and avarice, and thirst for national fame and glory.

The Reformation of the Church of England is anything but creditable to that church. I refer to Henry VIII., and the vacillating course taken by some of its early reformers; and its persecution of those who were opposed to it in religious faith.

I might here refer to the religious intolerance of Calvin of Geneva, and Knox of Scotland, and other reformers; but, as these are mere individual affairs, I pass over them. If we look at Christian nations as a whole, we see a picture that is truly lamentable, a miserable portrait of poor, degenerated, fallen humanity. We see Christian nations arrayed against Christian nations in battle, with the Christian ministers of each Christian nation calling upon the Christian's God to give them each the victory over their enemies! Christians! and worshippers of the same God!!

Hence, Christian England has been arrayed against Christian France; Christian Russia against Christian Prussia; Christian Spain against Christian Holland; Christian Austria against Christian Hungary; Christian England against Christian United States; and Christian United States against Christian Mexico. Not to mention the innumerable aggressions and conquests of some of the larger nations, not only upon their Christian brethren, but against other nations of the earth.

Before those several nations have engaged in their wars, their ministers have presented their several prayers before the same God; and if He had been as infatuated as they, and listened to their prayers, they would long ago have been destroyed, and the Christian world depopulated. After their prayers they have met in deadly strife; foe has rushed against foe with mortal energy, and the clarion of war, the clang of arms, and the cannon's roar have been followed by dying groans, shattered limbs, carnage, blood, and death; and unutterable misery and distress, desolate hearths, lonely widows, and fatherless children. And yet these are all Christian nations, Christian brethren, worshippers of the same God. Christianity has prevailed more or less for eighteen hundred years. If it should still continue and overspread the world in its present form, what would it accomplish? The world's redemption and regeneration? No, verily. Its most staunch supporters, and most strenuous advocates would say, *No*. For like causes always produce like effects: and if it has failed to regenerate the nations where it has had full sway for generations, it must necessarily fail to regenerate the world. If it has failed in a small thing, how can it accomplish a large one?

There are some of the Evangelical Churches, and modern reformers who will tell me that the above is not Christianity; only a form, not the spirit and life. But it is national Christianity; and it is the nations—the world and its redemption—that we are speaking of. But, lest they should think me unfair in making this application, I will briefly examine their position. Which of the sects or parties is it that is good, evangelical, and pure? The Church of England, Methodists, Presbyterians, Independents, Baptists, Universalists, or which of the hundreds of sects that flood Christendom? For they do not agree; there exists as much unhappy difference among them as there does among the nations. They have not power, of course, to act nationally; but, as individual sects, there is as much virulence, discord, division, and strife among them as among any other people. There is sect against sect; party against party; polemical essay against polemical essay; discussion after discussion; and hard words, bitter feelings, angry disputes, wrangling, hatred, and malice, prevail to an alarming extent: and it is enough, in many instances, for a member even of a family to be of a different religious persuasion, no matter how honest, to cause his expulsion from the family.

In fact, if we look at Christianity, as exhibited among the evangelical societies of England, and the United States, where Protestantism bears rule unchecked, what do we see? Nothing but a game at hazard, where a thousand opinions distract the people, each clamoring for his own peculiar form of worship, and, like the Athenians, clinging with tenacity to their own favorite god, no matter how absurd or ridiculous his pretensions. I would remark, however, both to Catholic and Protestant, that there is much good associated with both their systems, in the teaching of morality, virtue, faith in God, and our Lord Jesus Christ; that there are thousands of sincere, honest, good, and virtuous people among them, as also among the nations; that these evils have been the growth of ages. "The fathers have eaten sour grapes, and the children's teeth have been set on edge."

It is unnecessary here to say anything of missionary societies, tract societies, and evangelical societies; for if the fountain is impure, the stream must be impure; if the tree is bad, the fruit will be bad also. It is certainly a praiseworthy object to spread the Bible, and all useful information, and to do good as far as we can; but to talk of this evangelizing the world, is folly.

We will now turn our attention for a short time to another society, which has been formed lately in Europe, called a "Peace Society," and which has lately held several congresses in London, Berlin, and elsewhere, with representatives from many of the European nations, and the United States. Their object is, to ameliorate the condition of the world, and bring about universal peace; but, with all deference to their feelings, and fervent desires that such a happy event might be consummated, I must beg leave to differ from them in their views. Peace is a desirable thing; it is the gift of God, and the greatest gift that God can bestow upon mortals. What is more desirable than peace? Peace in nations, peace in cities, peace in families. Like the soft murmuring zephyr, its soothing influence calms the brow of care, dries the eye of sorrow, and chases trouble from the bosom; and let it be universally experienced, and it would drive sorrow from the world, and make this earth a paradise. But peace is the gift of God. Jesus said to his disciples, "Peace I leave with you; my peace I give unto you, not as the world giveth give I unto you." John xiv. 27. Moral suasion is always good, and the most happy that man can employ; but without the interposition of God, it will be useless.

The nations of the world have corrupted themselves before God, and we are not in a position to be governed by those principles without regeneration. If they were pure, and living in the fear of God, it would be another thing; but the world at the present time is not made of the proper materials to submit to a congressional interposition, of a kind similar to the one now established. The materials will not combine, and no power, short of the power of God, can accomplish it. We have got into the feet and toes of Daniel's national image; they are composed of iron and clay, which will not mix; there is no chemical affinity between the bodies. As it has been in generations past, the strong nations feel independent, and capable of taking care of their own affairs; and if the weak unite, it is to protect themselves against the strong. The principles of aggression and protection still rule as strong in the human bosom as ever they did. The world is as belligerent now as it ever was, and as full of commotion and uncertainty.

The dispositions of the nations, of kings, rulers, and people, are the same. The late revolutions in Europe, and present uncertain state of political affairs, are an evident proof of this. The political atmosphere of the European nations is full of combustion, and only needs igniting to set the whole in one common blaze. Talk of peace! there is war in the councils and cabinets, uncertainty and distrust with emperors, kings, presidents, and princes; war in the churches, clubs, cabals, and parties that now distract the world. It is whispered in the midnight caucus, and proclaimed in open day. The same spirit enters into the social circle, and breaks up families: father is arrayed against son, and son against father; mother against daughter, and daughter against mother; and brother against brother: it presides triumphant at the assemblies of the "Peace Society," and spreads confusion, discord, and division there. A moral, deadly, evil has infused itself throughout the world, and it needs a more powerful restorative than the one proposed to ameliorate its condition. If the root of the evil be not eradicated, in vain we regulate the branches; if the fountain be impure, in vain we strive to purify the streams. The means used are not adequate to the end designed, and in spite of all those weak, puny efforts, the world will continue in its present sickly state, unless a more powerful antidote be applied.

Another principle has many advocates on the Continent of Europe at the present time; a principle of Socialism. Like everything else, it is possessed of different phases, and has been advocated in its various branches by Fourier, Robert Owen, Cabet, Pierre Leroux, and Proudhon, in Europe, and Fanny Wright in America. The leading object of many of these people is to have a community of goods and property. Some of them discard Christianity altogether, and others leave every one to do as they please; others attach a little importance to it. I would briefly remark on the first of those, that if scepticism is to be the basis of the happiness of man, we shall be in a poor situation to improve the world. It is practical infidelity that has placed the world in its present position; how far the unblushing profession of it will lead to restoration and happiness, I must leave my readers to judge. It is our departure from God, that has brought upon us all our misery. It is not a very reasonable way to alleviate it by confirming mankind in scepticism. I am aware that there is much in the world to induce doubt, and uncertainty on religious affairs, and religious professors have much to answer for; but there is a very material difference between the religion of God, and our Lord Jesus Christ, and that of those who profess His name.

As regards Communism, in the abstract, or on the voluntary principle, we will examine that briefly. Pick out a number of men in Paris, London, Berlin, or any other city, associated with all the evils and corruptions of those cities, and organize them into a community. Will the mere removal of them from one place to another make them better? Certainly not. If they were corrupt before, they will be after their removal; and if they were unhappy before, they will be after. This temporary change will not make a difference; for men in possession of different religious, and political, and moral views, never can be united in harmony. The difficulties that exist in the world on a large scale, would exist there in miniature; and though prudence, forbearance, and policy, in smaller circles, might operate for a time, the evils would still exist; and though they might smoulder and be pent up, like a volcano, they would only rage with greater fury when they did burst out.

I have conversed with some who seem to think that all that is necessary to promote the happiness of man, is, that he have sufficient to eat and drink, and that through this means it would be obtained. I grant that the comforts and happiness of men are in a great measure augmented by these things; but to place them as the root and foundation, is wrong. In the present situation of Europe, where so much squalid poverty, wretchedness, and distress abound, it is not to be wondered at that such feelings should obtain. But, if we cast our eyes abroad in the world, we shall find that unhappiness is not always associated with the poor: it revels in the church and state; among kings, potentates, princes, and rulers: it follows the haunts of the libertine and profligate, and gnaws in many instances the conscience of the minister: it rides with lords and ladies in their carriages and chariots, and revels in splendid saloons and in banquet halls. Many a pleasant countenance covers an aching heart, and many a gorgeous costume hides the deadly worm; jealousy, disappointed ambition, blasted hopes, cold neglect, and conjugal infidelity, produce many a miserable heart; and rage, envy, malice, and murder, lurk in many instances under the cover of pomp, splendor, competency, or magnificence; not to mention the care, anxiety, and trouble of officers of state in these troublous times. If the poor knew the situation of many of those in different circumstances, they would not envy their situations.

Again, if we notice the position of some of the southern and western States of America. They have abundance to eat and to drink, their lands bring forth bountifully. But does this make them happy? Verily, no. The same false state of society exists there; men are awfully under the influence of their depraved passions; men are frequently put to death by what is called "Lynch law," without judge or jury. The pistol, the bowie knife, the rifle, and the dirk, are in frequent requisition, and misery and unhappiness prevail.

In Mexico, where they possess one of the richest countries in the world, a salubrious climate, a rich soil, abounding also with the most valuable mineral resources, yet the people are unhappy. Guerillas plunder the traveller, their streets are crowded with beggars; its men are without courage or energy, and the country is left a prey to any nation, who has covetousness or power to oppress it. The Scriptures say, that "Man shall not live by bread alone, but by every word that proceedeth from the mouth of God;" and as they do not exist in this way, another Scripture tells the story in plain terms, for it says, "Where there is no vision the people perish." Proverbs xxix. 18.

There is also another political party, who desire, through the influence of legislation and coercion, to level the world. To say the least, it is a species of robbery; to some it may appear an honorable one, but, nevertheless, it is robbery. What right has any private man to take by force the property of another? The laws of all nations would punish such a man as a thief. Would thousands of men engaged in the same business make it more honorable? Certainly not. And if a nation were to do it, would a nation's act sanctify a wrong deed? No; the Algerine pirates, or Arabian hordes, were never considered honorable, on account of their numbers; and a nation, or nations, engaging in this would only augment the banditti, but could never sanctify the deed. I shall not, here, enter into the various manners of obtaining wealth; but would merely state, that any unjust acquisition of it ought to be punished by law. Wealth is generally the representation of labour, industry, and talent. If one man is industrious, enterprising, diligent, careful, and saves property, and his children follow in his steps, and accumulate wealth; and another man is careless, prodigal, and lazy, and his children inherit his poverty, I cannot conceive upon what principles of justice, the children of the idle and profligate have a right to put their hands into the pockets of those who are diligent and careful, and rob them of their purse. Let this principle exist, and all energy and enterprise would be crushed. Men would be afraid of again accumulating, lest they should again be robbed. Industry and talent would have no stimulant, and confusion and ruin would inevitably follow. Again, if you took men's property without their consent, the natural consequence would be that they would seek to retake it the first opportunity; and this state of things would only deluge the world in blood. So that let any of these measures be carried out, even according to the most sanguine hopes of the parties, they would not only bring distress upon others, but also upon themselves; certainly they would not bring about the peace of the world.

One thing more upon this subject, and I have done. In Europe, there has been of late years a great mania for revolutions—a strong desire to establish republican governments; but let me remark here, that the form of government will not materially affect the position of the people, nor add to the resources of a country. If a country is rich and prosperous under a monarchy, it will be so under a republic, and *vice versa*. If poor under one, it will be under another. If nations think proper to change their form of government, they of course have a right to do so; but to think that this will ameliorate their condition, and produce happiness, is altogether a mistake. Happiness and peace are the gifts of God, and come from Him. Every kind of government has its good and evil properties. Rome was unhappy under a kingly government, and also under a republican form. Carthage as a republic was no more happy than many of its monarchial contemporaries; nor was Corinth, Holland, or Venice; and republican Genoa has not manifested anything very much in favor of these principles. France was unhappy under her emperor, she was unhappy under her kings, and is unhappy as a republic. America is perhaps some little exception to this; but the difference lies not so much in her government, as in the extent of her country, the richness of her soil, and abundance of her resources; for, as I have already mentioned, "Lynch law" prevails to an alarming extent in the south and west. In the state of New York, in the east, there are mobs painted as Indians resisting the officers of the law, and doing it with impunity; and it is a matter of doubt whether persons having paid for property, shall own it, or be dispossessed by their tenants, not in law, for the constitution and laws are good, but in practice defective, through popular clamor and violence. I refer to the estates of Van Ranseller and others; and, in the west, to Joseph and Hyrum Smith, who were murdered in Carthage jail, without any redress, although their murderers were known to the officers of state; and to the inhabitants of a city, ten thousand in number, together with twenty thousand others, principally farmers, labourers, and mechanics, occupying a country about ten miles wide, and thirty long, most of which was well cultivated and owned by the occupants,—who were all forced by continual harassing by lawless mobs, to leave a country in which they could not be protected, and seek an asylum in a far off desert home, there being no power in the government to give redress.

It is altogether an infatuation to think that a change in government will mend the circumstances, or increase the resources, when the whole world is groaning under corruption. If there are twenty men who have twenty pounds of bread to divide amongst them, it matters but little whether it is divided by three, ten, or the whole, it will not increase the amount. I grant, however, that there are flagrant abuses, of which we have mentioned some, associated with all kinds of governments, and many things to be complained of justly; but they arise from the wickedness of man, and the corrupt and artificial state of society. Do away with one set of rulers, and you have only the same materials to make another of; and if ever so honestly disposed, they are surrounded with such a train of circumstances, over which they have no control, that they cannot mend them.

There is frequently much excitement on this subject; and many people ignorant of these things, are led to suppose that their resources will be increased, and their circumstances bettered; but when they find, after much contention, struggling, and bloodshed, that it does not rain bread, cheese, and clothing; that it is only a change of men, papers, and parchment, chagrin and disappointment naturally follow. There is much that is good, and much that is bad in all governments; and I am not seeking here to portray a perfect government, but to show some of the evils associated with them, and the utter incompetency of all the plans of men to restore a perfect government; and as all their plans have failed, so they will fail, for it is the work of God, and not of man. The moral agency of man without God, has had its full development; his weakness, wickedness, and corruption, have placed the world where it is: he can see as in a glass his incompetency, and folly, and nothing but the power of God can restore it.

It is not to be wondered at, that those various plans should exist, for the world is in a horrible situation. Jesus prophesied of it, and said, there should be upon the earth "distress of nations, perplexity, men's hearts failing them, for fear, and for looking after those things which are coming upon the earth," Luke xxi. 25, 26. Men see these things, and their hearts fear; confusion, disorder, misery, blood, and ruin, seem to stare them in the face; and in the absence of something great, noble, and magnificent, suited to the exigency of the case, they try the foregoing remedies, as a sailor, in the absence of a boat, would cling with tenacity to any floating piece of wreck, to save him from a watery grave.

Neither can men be blamed for trying to do good; it is certainly a laudable object; and with all the selfishness, ambition, and pride, associated with the foregoing, it must be admitted that there is much uprightness, sincerity, and honest zeal.

There are very many philanthropists who would gladly ameliorate the condition of men, and of the world, if they knew how. But the means employed are not commensurate with the end; every grade of society is vitiated and corrupt. "The whole head is sick, and the whole heart faint." Our systems, our policy, our legislation, our education, and philosophy, are all wrong, neither can we be particularly blamed, for these evils have been the growth of ages. Our fathers have left God, his guidance, control, and support, and we have been left to ourselves; and our present position is a manifest proof of our incompetency to govern; and our past failures make it evident, that any future effort, with the same means, would be as useless. The world is diseased, and it requires a world's remedy.

Chapter IV.

What Is Man? What Is His Destiny and Relationship to God?

Having shewn in the foregoing chapters, that the rule of God is perfect where he governs alone, that the rule of man is imperfect, and has introduced confusion and misery, and that the plans of men are not competent to restore the world to happiness, and the fulfilment of the object for which it was created; it now devolves upon us to investigate the way that this thing can, and will be accomplished; for there is a time spoken of in the Scriptures, when there will be a reign of righteousness.

First, then, we will enquire who and what is man? and what is his destiny, and what his relationship to God? For before we can define government correctly, it will be necessary to find out the nature of the being that has to be governed.

What, then, is man? Is he a being temporal and earthly alone, and when he dies, does he sink into forgetfulness? Is he annihilated? or has he a spirit as well as a body? If the first be the case, he alone has a right to regulate his own affairs, to frame his own government, and to pursue that course which to him seems good; if not, the case is different. I do not here wish to enter into a philosophical disquisition on the subject, but, as I am writing at present to believers in the Bible, I shall confine myself more to that. I will state, that man is an eternal being, composed of body and spirit: his spirit existed before he came here; his body exists with the spirit in time, and after death the spirit exists without the body. In the resurrection, both body and spirit will finally be reunited; and it requires both body and spirit to make a perfect man, whether in time, or eternity.

I know there are those who suppose that the spirit of man comes into existence with his body, and that intelligence and spirit are organized with the body; but we read, that when God made man, he made him of the dust of the earth; he made him in his own likeness. Man was then a lifeless body; He afterwards "breathed into him the breath of life, and man became a living soul."

Before that spirit was given, he was dead, lifeless; and when that spirit is taken away, he is again lifeless; and let not any one say that the body is perfect without the spirit; for the moment the spirit leaves the body, no matter how perfect its organization may be, the man is inanimate, and destitute of intelligence and feeling: "it is the spirit that gives life." Hence we find that when Jarius's daughter was dead, his servant came and told him, saying, "Thy daughter is dead, trouble not the master;" but when she was restored, it is said "her spirit *came again*, and she arose straightway." Luke viii. 55. When her spirit was absent, the body was dead; when it returned, the body lived. "Moses spake unto the Lord, and said, let the Lord, the God of *the spirits of all flesh*, set a man over the congregation." Num. xxvii. 16. Again, the Lord in speaking to Jeremiah, said, "Before I formed thee in the belly, I knew thee," i. 5. I would ask, What part of Jeremiah did he know? It could not be his body, for it was not in existence; but he knew his spirit, for "he was the father of his spirit."

The Lord speaks to Job and says, "Where wast thou when I laid the foundations of the earth? declare if thou hast understanding, who hath laid the measures thereof, if thou knowest? or who hath stretched the line upon it. Whereupon are the foundations thereof fastened? or who laid the corner stone thereof? when the morning stars sung together, and all the sons of God shouted for joy?" xxxviii. 4, 6. Again, John says, "They that dwell on the earth, shall wonder, whose names were not written in the book of life from the foundation of the world." Rev. xvii. 8.

This spirit proceeds forth from God, and is eternal; hence Solomon says, in speaking of death, "Then shall the dust return to the earth as it was, and the spirit unto God who gave it." Eccles. xii. 7. That the spirit is eternal, is very evident, from the Scriptures; Jesus prayed to his father, and said, "O Father, glorify thou me, with thine own self, with the glory which I had with thee *before the world was.*" John xvii. 5. Here Jesus speaks of an existence before he came here, of a glory he had with his Father before the world was. Christ, then, existed before he came here and took a body. Again Jesus says, "I have manifested thy name unto the men which thou gavest me out of the world: thine they were, and thou gavest them me." John xvii. 6.

Let us see what the Apostle Paul says on the subject: "Blessed be the God and Father of our Lord Jesus Christ, who hath blessed us with all spiritual blessings, in heavenly places, in Christ; according as he hath chosen us in him, before the foundation of the world." Ephes. i, 3, 4. Christ, then, existed with his Father before the world was, and the Saints existed in, or with him. What part? their bodies? no, their spirits. Again, man exists after he leaves here. It is unnecessary to say anything about the life of the spirit, after the death of the body, or of the resurrection, as the subjects are so generally known and believed. Paul says, "If in this life only, we have hope in Christ, we are of all men most miserable. But now is Christ risen from the dead, and become the first fruits of them that slept. For since by man came death, by man came also the resurrection of the dead. ... The trumpet shall sound, and the dead shall be raised incorruptible, and we shall be changed; for this corruptible must put on incorruption, and this mortal must put on immortality, then shall be brought to pass the saying that is written, Death is swallowed up in victory." 1 Cor. xv. 19-21, 52-54.

If man, then, is an eternal being, came from God, exists here for a short time, and will return, it is necessary that he know something about God, and his government. For he has to do with him not only in time, but in eternity, and whatever man may be disposed to do, or however he may vaunt himself of his own abilities, there are some things he has no control over. He came into the world without his agency, he will have to leave it, whether he desires it or not; and he will also have to appear in another world. He is destined, if he improves his opportunities, to higher and greater blessings and glory than are associated with this earth in its present state: and hence the necessity of the guidance of a superior power, and intelligence, that he may not act the part of a fool here, and jeopardize his eternal interests; but that his intelligence may be commensurate with his position; that his actions here may have a bearing upon his future destiny; that he may not sink into the slough of iniquity and degradation, and contaminate himself with corruption; that he may stand pure, virtuous, intelligent, and honourable, as a son of God, and seek for, and be guided and governed by his Father's counsels. Having said so much on this subject, we will continue our investigation still further, and enquire next, What is our relationship to God? In answering this, I would briefly remark, that the position that we stand in to him, is that of a son. Adam is the father of our bodies, and God is the father of our spirits. I know that some are in the habit of looking upon God, as a monster only to be dreaded, known only in the earthquake, the tempest, the thunder, and the storm, and that there is something gloomy and dismal attached to his service. If there is, it is the appendage of man, and not of God. Is there anything gloomy in the works that God has made? Turn where we will, we see harmony, loveliness, cheerfulness, and beauty.

The blessings of providence were made for man, and his enjoyment; he is placed as head of creation. For him the earth teems with the richest profusion; the golden grain, the luscious fruit, the choicest vines; for him, the herbs, and flowers, bedeck the earth, shed their odoriferous perfumes, and display their gorgeous beauty; for him, the proud horse yields his back, the cow gives her milk, and the bee its honey; for him, the sheep yields its fleece, the cotton-tree its down, and the worm its silk. For him, the shrub and vine bloom and blossom, and nature clothes herself in her richest attire; the rippling stream, the pure fountain, the crystal river flow for him, all nature spreads her richest charms, and invites him to partake of her joyousness, beauty, and innocence, and to worship her God.

Talk about melancholy, in the fear of God, and in his service! It is the corruption of the world, that has made men unhappy; and the corruption of religion that has made it gloomy: these are the miseries entailed by men, not the blessings of God. Talk about gloom! is there gloom in the warbling of the birds, in the prancing of the horse, in the playfulness of the lamb, or kid; in the beauty of flowers, in any of Nature's gifts, or rich attire, or in God, that made them, or in his service?

There are others, again, who would place the Lord at an immense distance, and render our approach to him almost impossible; but this is a superstitious idea, for our Father listens to the cries of his children, numbers the hairs of their heads; and the Scriptures say, "a sparrow cannot fall to the ground, without his notice." He speaks to his elect, and says, "He that toucheth you, toucheth the apple of his eye." Zech. ii. 8. He is our Father; and hence the Scriptures tell us to pray, "Our Father, who art in heaven." Paul says, "We have had fathers of our flesh, which corrected us, and we gave them reverence; shall we not much rather be in subjection unto the Father of spirits, and live?" Heb. xii. 9. We have, then, both a temporal and a spiritual Father; and hence his solicitude for our welfare, and his desire for our happiness. Says Jesus, "If a son ask bread, will he for bread give him a stone? or if he ask a fish, will he give him a serpent. If ye, then, being evil, know how to give good gifts unto your children, how much more shall your Father which is in heaven, give good things to them that ask him."

What a delightful reflection for his servants, to draw nigh to their Father, as to an endearing parent, and ask for blessings, as a son would ask for bread, and be confident of receiving. Hence the faithful in the Apostles' days received a spirit, whereby they could say, "Abba, Father," or Father, Father. What an endearing relationship! and if the world could comprehend, how gladly would they throw themselves upon his guardianship, seek his wisdom and government, and claim a father's benediction; but Satan has blinded the eyes of the world, and they know not the things which make for their peace.

Chapter V.

The Object of Man's Existence on the Earth; and His Relationship Thereto.

We next enquire, What is the object and design of man's existence on the earth; and what is his relationship thereto? for all this magnificent world, with its creation, life, beauty, symmetry, order, and grandeur, could not be without design; and as God existed before man, there must have been some object in man's creation, and in his appearance on the earth. As I have before stated, man existed before he came here, in a spiritual substance, but had not a body; when I speak of a body, I mean an earthly one, for I consider the spirit is substance, but more elastic, subtle, and refined than the fleshy body; that in the union of the spirit and flesh, there is more perfection than in the spirit alone. The body is not perfect without the spirit, nor the spirit without the body; it takes the two to make a perfect man, for the spirit requires a tabernacle, to give it power to develop itself and to exalt it in the scale of intelligence, both in time and eternity. One of the greatest curses inflicted on Satan and his followers, when they were cast out of heaven, was, that they should have no body. Hence, when he appeared before the Lord, and was asked from whence he came, he answered, "From going to and fro in the earth, and from walking up and down in it." Job i. 7, and ii. 2. For this reason he is denominated "The Prince of the power of the air, the Spirit that now worketh in the children of disobedience." Ephes. ii. 2. Hence he exerts an invisible agency over the spirits of men, darkens their minds, and uses his infernal power to confound, corrupt, destroy and envelope the world in confusion, misery, and distress; and, although deprived personally of operating with a body, he uses his influence over the spirits of those who have bodies, to resist goodness, virtue, purity, intelligence, and the fear of God; and consequently, the happiness of man; and poor erring humanity is made the dupe of his wiles. The Apostle says, "The God of this world hath blinded the minds of them which believe not, lest the light of the glorious gospel of Christ who is the image of God, should shine unto them." 2 Cor. iv. 4. But not content with the ravages he has made, the spoliation, misery, and distress, not having a tabernacle of his own, he has frequently sought to occupy that of man, in order that he might yet possess greater power, and more fully accomplish the devastation. We read, that in our Saviour's days, there were persons possessed with devils, who were tormented by them; and Jesus and his disciples cast them out. Mary Magdalene was dispossessed of seven. A legion had entered one man, and when commanded to leave, rather than have no bodies, they desired permission to enter those of swine, which they did, and the swine were destroyed. Man's body to him, then, is of great importance, and if he only knew and appreciated his privileges, he might live above the temptation of Satan, the influence of corruption, subdue his lusts, overcome the world, and triumph, and enjoy the blessings of God, in time and in eternity.

The object of man's taking a body is, that through the redemption of Jesus Christ, both soul and body may be exalted in the eternal world, when the earth shall be celestial, and to obtain a higher exaltation than he would be capable of doing without a body. For when man was first made, he was made "a little lower than the angels," Heb. ii. 7; but through the atonement and resurrection of Jesus Christ, he is placed in a position to obtain an exaltation higher than that of angels. Says the Apostle, "Know ye not that we shall judge angels?" 1 Cor. vi. 3. "Jesus descended below all things, that he might be raised above all things." He took upon him a body, that he might die as a man, and "that through death, he might destroy him that had the power of death, that is, the Devil." Heb. ii. 14. Having conquered Death, then, in his own dominions, burst the barriers of the tomb, and ascended with his body triumphant to the right hand of God, he has accomplished a purpose which God had decreed from before the foundation of the world, "and opened the kingdom of heaven to all believers." Hence man, through obedience to the Gospel, is placed in a position to be an adopted son of God, and have a legitimate right to his Father's blessings, and to possess the gift of the Holy Ghost. And the Apostle says, that "If the spirit of him that raised up Jesus from the dead, dwell in you, he that raised up Christ from the dead shall also quicken your mortal bodies by his Spirit that dwelleth in you." Rom. viii. 11. Thus, as Jesus vanquished death, so may we; as he overcame, so may we; and, if faithful, sit with him upon his throne, as he has overcome, and sat down upon his Father's throne. Rev. iii. 21. Thus, man will not only be raised from degradation, but will also be exalted to a seat among the intelligences which surround the throne of God. This is one great object of our coming here and taking bodies.

Another object that we came here for, and took bodies, was to propagate our species. For if it is for our benefit to come here, it is also for the benefit of others. Hence the first commandment given to man was, "Be fruitful and multiply, and replenish the earth, and subdue it." Gen. i. 28. And as man is an eternal being, and all his actions have a relevancy to eternity, it is necessary that he understand his position well, and thus fulfil the measure of his creation. For as he, and his offspring are destined to live eternally, he is not only responsible for his own acts, but in a great measure for those of his children, in framing their minds, regulating their morals, setting them a correct example, and teaching them correct principles; but more especially in preserving the *purity* of his own body. And why? Because, if he abuses his body, and corrupts himself, he not only injures himself, but his partner and associates, and entails misery incalculable upon his posterity, who are doomed to inherit the father's misery; and this is not only associated with time, but with eternity. Hence the Lord has given laws regulating marriage and chastity of the strictest kind, and entailed the severest punishment upon those, who, in different ages have abused this sacred ordinance. For example, the curse of Sodom and Gomorrah: and the terrible judgments pronounced against those who should corrupt and defile their bodies, let any one read Deut. xxii. 13-30. And Paul says, "Know ye not that ye are the temple of God, and that the Spirit of God dwelleth in you? If any man defile the temple of God, him shall God destroy." 1 Cor. iii. 16, 17. Whoremongers and adulterers shall not enter into the kingdom of heaven. 1 Cor. vi. 9, 10; and Heb. xiii. 4. And why? Because man being made a free agent over his own body, that he might exalt himself and posterity, both in time and in eternity, if he abuses that power, he not only affects himself, but unborn bodies and spirits, corrupting the world, and opening the flood gates of vice, immorality, and estrangement from God. Hence the children of Israel were told not to marry with the surrounding nations, lest their seed should be corrupted, and the people turned to idolatry, which would lead to the forgetfulness of God, to an ignorance of his purposes and designs, and cause them to lose sight of the object of their creation, and corrupt themselves; and to the introduction of every other evil, as a natural consequence. But where the order of God is carried out, it places things in a lovely position.

What is more amiable and pleasant than those pure, innocent, endearing affections which God has placed in the hearts of the man and woman, who are united together in lawful matrimony? With a love and confidence pure as the love of God, because it springs from him, and is his gift; with bodies chaste, and virtuous; and an offspring, lovely, healthy, innocent, and uncontaminated; confiding in each other, they live together in the fear of God, enjoying nature's gifts uncorrupted and undefiled as the driven snow, or the crystal stream. But how would this enjoyment be enhanced, if they understood their destiny; could unravel the designs of God, and contemplate an eternal union, in another state of existence; a connexion with their offspring, commenced here to endure for ever, and all their ties, relationships, and affections strengthened! A mother feels great delight in beholding her child, and gazing on its lovely infant form. How would her bosom swell with ecstacy at the contemplation of that child being with her for ever! And if we only understood our position, this was the object for which we came into the world. And the object of the kingdom of God is, to re-establish all those holy principles.

Chastity and purity are things of the greatest importance to the world. Hence the Prophet says, "Because the Lord hath been witness between thee and the wife of thy youth, against whom thou hast dealt treacherously; yet is she thy companion, and the wife of thy covenant. And did not he make one? Yet had he the residue of the Spirit. And wherefore one? that he might *seek a godly seed*. Therefore take heed to your spirit, and let none deal treacherously against the wife of his youth." Mal. ii. 14, 15. Here, then, the object of purity is pointed out clearly; and what is it? that God might preserve a godly seed. St. Paul says, "What? know ye not that he who is joined to an harlot is one body? for two, saith he, shall be one flesh.... Flee fornication. Every sin that a man doeth is without the body; but he that committeth fornication, sinneth against his own body. What? know ye not that your body is the temple of the Holy Ghost which is in you, which ye have of God, and ye are not your own." 1 Cor. vi. 16-20. And in the next chapter he speaks of the same things which Malachi does concerning a pure seed. "For the unbelieving husband is sanctified by the wife, and the unbelieving wife is sanctified by the husband, else were your children unclean; *but now are they holy*."

The legislators of all civilized nations have seen the necessity of sustaining these things, and consequently have passed, generally, very rigid laws for the protection of female virtue, and the support of the marriage contract. Hence Acts have been passed and enforced, disinheriting those who were not born in wedlock. This, in some instances, has produced a salutary effect. Ministers of the various churches have also used their influence, in a great measure, in support of virtuous principles. These have had their effect in assisting to stem the torrent of iniquity. But as the nations themselves have forsaken God, how can they expect to stop this crying evil; for the very legislators who pass these laws are in many instances guilty themselves; and when kings, princes, and rulers, corrupt themselves, how can they expect the people to be pure? for no matter how rigid law may be, corrupt persons will always find means to evade it. And, indeed, so far have these abominations gone, that it seems to be an admitted fact, that these things cannot be controlled; and, although there are laws relative to matrimonial alliances, yet there are some nations, called Christian, who actually give licence for prostitution, and all the degradation and misery associated with it. Nor are these things connected with the lower ranks of life only; wantonness and voluptuousness go hand in hand, and revel unchecked in courts, among the nobles and kings of the earth. The statesman, the politician, and the merchant, the mechanic and the labourer, have all corrupted themselves. The world is full of adultery, intrigues, fornication, and abominations. Let any one go to the masked balls in the principal theatres in Paris, and he will see thousands of people of both sexes, impudently, shamelessly, and unblushingly, manifesting their lewd dispositions. Indeed, debauch and wantonness bear full sway, not to speak of the dens of abomination that exist elsewhere. London abounds with unfortunate beings, led on by example, seduction, and misery, to their fallen, degraded condition. The same thing exists throughout England, France, the United States, and all nations. Hence millions of youth corrupt themselves, engender the most loathsome diseases, and curse their posterity with their sin, who, in their turn, rise up and tread in the corrupt steps of their fathers. Not to say anything of the thousands of lovely beings whom God designed for companions of man in time and in eternity, and for raising up a pure offspring, who are corrupted, degraded, polluted, fallen, poor, miserable wretches; outcasts of society, insulted, oppressed, despised, and abused; dragging out a miserable existence; led on from one degree of degradation to another, till death, as a friend, closes their wretched career, and yet without hope. Thus, man that was made pure, in the image of his Maker, that could stand proudly erect as the representative of God, pure, and uncontaminated, is debased, fallen, corrupt, diseased, and sunk below the brute creation; a creature of lust and passion, and a slave to his unbridled appetites. I write plainly on this subject; and I do it because it is a curse to the world, and God will have a reckoning with the nations for these things. In vain, then, men legislate on these matters: the nations have corrupted themselves, and these things are beyond their control. Men must be governed by higher, and purer motives than merely human enactments. If the world understood its true position, and the eternal consequences to them and their seed, they would feel different. They would feel that they were eternal beings; that they were responsible to God, both for their bodies and spirits. Nothing but a knowledge of man's fall and true position, and the development of the kingdom of God, can restore him to his proper state, restore the order and economy of God, and place man again in his natural position on the earth.

Having spoken of man as an eternal being, we will now examine what relation he has to this earth; for it is the government of God that we wish to keep our minds upon. This earth is man's eternal inheritance, where he will exist after the resurrection, for it is destined to be purified and become celestial. I know that this position is considered strange by many, because it is generally supposed that we are going to heaven; that heaven is the final destination of the righteous; and that when we leave this world, we never return. Hence Wesley says—

"Beyond the bounds of time and space,

Look forward to that heavenly place,

The Saints' secure abode;"

and this is an opinion generally believed by the Christian world.

We shall therefore commence by enquiring, Where is heaven? Can any one point out its location? I would remark, that it is a word of almost unlimited signification; nevertheless we will investigate the matter a little. We read, that in the beginning "God created the heavens and the earth;" and furthermore, that he called the "firmament heaven." From the above we learn, that the heavens were created by the Lord, and that the heavens were created at, or about the same time as the earth, and that the firmament is called heaven. We are further told concerning the firmament, that "God separated the waters that were below the firmament, from those that were above the firmament."

Hence, when God destroyed the world with a flood, "He opened the windows of heaven;" when the rain ceased, he "shut the windows of heaven." Now, a word on this firmament; Where is it? "And God said, Let the waters bring forth abundantly the moving creature that hath life, and fowl that may fly above the earth in the open firmament of heaven." We find out, then, from the foregoing, that the firmament is called heaven, viz., the heaven associated with this earth; and that the firmament is the place where the birds fly, and the rain falls from heaven; and the scriptures say, that Jesus will come in the clouds of heaven. Matt. xxiv. 30. Mark xiii. 26. But there are other heavens: for God created this heaven, and this earth; and his throne existed before this world rolled into existence, or the morning stars sang together for joy; for "Heaven is God's throne, and the earth is his footstool." Solomon says, "The heaven of heavens cannot contain thee." This heaven is veiled from mortal vision; spirits abound, but we cannot see them; and angels hover there, but to us are invisible, and can only be known or seen by the revelation of God. Hence Paul says, he "was caught up into the *third* heaven." Stephen "saw the heavens opened, and Jesus sitting on the right hand of God." Where this revelation exists, there exists without the removal of the body a perfect knowledge of things as they are known to God, so far as they are revealed. Thus, when John was on the Isle of Patmos, he says, "I was in the spirit on the Lord's day, and heard behind me a great voice, as of a trumpet, Saying, I am Alpha and Omega, the first and the last, and What thou seest write in a book." Rev. i. 10, 11. Then commenced the revelation. It was the same also with Stephen. From this we gather, that there is a veil that obscures the heavens from our sight; but when that veil is removed, and our vision is enlightened by the spirit of God, then we can gaze upon the glories of the eternal world, and heaven is opened for our view.

When persons are taken from the earth, and hid from our view, it is said they are gone to heaven. Hence it is said, that Elijah went by a whirlwind into heaven, 2 Kings ii. 11. And it is also said of Jesus that "while he blessed them he was parted from them, and carried up into heaven." Luke xxiv. 51. But it is the destination of the Saints that we have to do with; and on this I would remark, that there are many glories, and man will be judged according to his deeds. "There is one glory of the sun, and another glory of the moon, and another glory of the stars; for as one star differeth from another star in glory, so also is the resurrection." 2 Cor. xv. 41, 42.

It would not comport with my object at the present time to enter into the whole of the details of this subject. I would briefly remark, however, inasmuch as I am now talking of man's body, that there is a place called "Paradise," to which the spirits of the dead go, awaiting the resurrection, and their reunion with the body. This was an old doctrine of the Jews. Paul, too, "was caught up into paradise and heard unspeakable words." 2 Cor. xii. 4. John says, "to him that overcometh will I grant to eat of the tree of life, which is in the midst of the paradise of God." Rev. ii. 7. This Paradise, however, is not the place for resurrected bodies, but for departed spirits: for Jesus said to the thief on the cross, "To day shalt thou be with me in Paradise." Luke xxiii. 43. Two days after this, and after the resurrection of his body, Mary was looking for the Lord, and he appeared to her: he said to her "Touch me not, for I am not yet ascended to my Father; but go to my brethren, and say unto them, I ascend unto my Father and your Father; and to my God, and your God." John xx. 17. We learn here, then, that Jesus went to Paradise, with the thief on the cross, in spirit; but that he had not been with his body to his Father.

We will now speak of heaven, as a place of reward for the righteous. Daniel, in speaking of the resurrection, says,

"Many of them that sleep in the dust of the earth shall awake; some to everlasting life, and some to shame and everlasting contempt." Dan. xii. 2. Jesus says, those who have forsaken all and followed him, "shall inherit everlasting life" Matt. xix. 29.

There is also a Book of Life spoken of. Paul speaks of some whose names were written therein. Phil. iv. 3. John also refers to the same things: he says "He that overcometh, the same shall be clothed in white raiment; and I will not blot out his name out of the Book of Life." Rev. iii. 5. Again, John, in speaking of the New Jerusalem, says, There shall not enter into it anything that worketh abomination, or maketh a lie; but they which are written in the Lamb's Book of Life. Rev. xxi. 27. From this it would appear, that those who obey all the commandments of God, and have their names written in the Lamb's Book of Life, shall finally enter into the New Jerusalem. Jesus again says, "To him that overcometh will I grant to sit with me in my throne, even as I also overcame, and am sat down with my Father in his throne." Rev. iii. 21. This, then, is the heaven, as far as I can conceive, that people expect to go to.

We will now try to find out its location. Above we have noticed that the saints are to have everlasting life, that they are to be with Jesus, and also in the New Jerusalem. We have now to enquire, Where Jesus's kingdom will be, and Where will be the place of the New Jerusalem. Daniel says, "I saw in the night visions, and behold one like the son of man came with the clouds of heaven, and came to the Ancient of Days, and they brought him near before him. And there was given him dominion, and glory, and a kingdom, that all people, nations, and languages, should serve him: his dominion is an everlasting dominion, which shall not pass away, and his kingdom that which shall not be destroyed." Dan. vii. 13, 14. Here, then, we find Jesus coming to establish a kingdom. Where is that kingdom? The Scriptures say, that all nations, languages, and tongues shall serve and obey him. Where do those nations, languages, and tongues exist? The answer is, on the earth. We will next enquire, Where the saints will be. Daniel says, in the 27th verse, "And the kingdom, and dominion, and the greatness of the kingdom under the *whole heaven* shall be given to the people of the saints of the Most High." Here, then, we find Jesus reigning under the whole heaven with his saints, and all nations, dominions, and powers, serving him. I noticed above, that those who overcame would be with Jesus, and with him have everlasting life. Zechariah speaks of a time when there will be a great assemblage of people against Jerusalem; after God's ancient people, the Jews, shall have been gathered there, and the Lord himself shall come forth to their defence. He says, "Then shall the Lord go forth, and fight against those nations, as when he fought in the day of battle. And his feet shall stand in that day upon the Mount of Olives, which is before Jerusalem on the east; and the Mount of Olives shall cleave in the midst thereof, toward the east and toward the west, and there shall be a very great valley; and half of the mountain shall remove toward the north, and half of it toward the south. And ye shall flee to the valley of the mountains; for the valley of the mountains shall reach unto Azal; yea, ye shall flee, like as ye fled from before the earthquake in the days of Uzziah, king of Judah: and the Lord my God shall come and all the saints with thee. And the Lord shall be king *over all the earth*: in that day there shall be one Lord, and his name one." xiv. 3, 4, 5, 9. Here we find that Jesus is to come, and *all his saints* are to come with him. And that the Lord is to be King over *all the earth*. The question again arises, Where will Jesus reign with his saints? the answer is, *upon the earth*. Again, we will refer to the revelations of John. He says, "I saw the souls of them that were beheaded for the witness of Jesus and for the word of God .... and they lived and reigned with Christ a thousand years," Rev. xx. 4. And if we wish to know Where they will reign, we will again let John speak: "For thou wast slain, and hast redeemed us to God by thy blood, out of every kindred, and tongue, and people, and nation. And hast made us unto our God kings and priests, and we shall reign *on the earth*." Rev. v. 9, 10. It is not necessary to quote more on this subject; it is so plain that he that runs may read. I know that there are those who will tell us that this is not the final destination of the saints. I would here remark, that a great many events will take place in regard to the renovation of the earth, which it would be foreign to my subject at the present time to detail. I would state, however, that when the earth shall have become pure, if people suppose that they will then inhabit a heaven, not on the earth, they are mistaken; for if we have the good fortune to have our names written in the Lamb's Book of Life, and to enter into the New Jerusalem, we shall in that very New Jerusalem have to descend to the earth. Methinks I hear persons saying, What! shall we not, then, stay in heaven? Yes—in heaven; but that heaven will be on the earth; for John says, "And I saw a new heaven and a new earth; for the first heaven and the first earth were past away (purified by fire and become celestial), and there was no more sea. And I John saw the holy city, New Jerusalem, coming down from God out of heaven, prepared as a bride adorned for her husband. And I heard a great voice out of heaven, saying, Behold the tabernacle of God is with men, and he will dwell with them, and they shall be his people, and God himself shall be with them, and be their God. And God shall wipe away all tears from their eyes; and there shall be no more death, neither sorrow, nor crying, neither shall there be any more pain; for the former things are passed away." Rev. xxi. 1-4. Here, then, we find man's final dwelling place is the earth; and for this purpose it was first created, and it never will fulfil the measure of its creation until this shall take place. Nor will man ever attain to the end for which he was created, till his spirit and his body are purified, and he takes his proper position on the earth.

The prophets of God, in every age, have looked forward to this time; and while many considered them to be fools, they were laying for themselves an eternal foundation: they looked with scorn upon the gaudy baubles that fascinated foolish and corrupt man: they could not yield to his chicanery and deception; but with the fear of God before their eyes, and a knowledge of the future, they stood proudly erect, in a consciousness of their innocence and integrity; despised alike the praise and powers of men, endured afflictions, privations, and death; wandered in sheep skins and goat skins, destitute, tormented, and afflicted, for "they looked for a city which hath foundations, whose builder and maker is God." Heb. xi. 10. Hence Job says, "I know that my Redeemer liveth, and that he shall stand at the latter day *upon the earth*; and though after my skin worms destroy this body, yet in my flesh shall I see God." xix. 25, 26. Man naturally clings to this earth; there seems to be something inherent in his nature that draws and binds his affections to the earth; hence he strives all that lays in his power to possess as much land as he can reasonably obtain; and not always honestly, but wars have been waged for the acquisition of territory, and the possessions of the earth. But what avails it all without God! So far from benefiting man, it is an injury, if obtained by fraud; for he has got to pass that test which none can avoid. And if circumstances here give him the power over his brother, when he leaves this world and appears before God, he goes to be judged for that very act of oppression; and the thing that he so anxiously desired to obtain in this world is his curse in the next. An honourable desire for property is not wrong; but no man can have a lasting claim unless it is given him of God. Lands, properties, possessions, and the blessings of this life, are of use only as they are sanctified, and have a bearing on the world to come. There have been hereditary laws established in England, and I believe in other countries, securing landed possessions to the eldest son, or heir. This has originated from the above feeling; and partly from the customs of the ancient Israelites, as recorded in the Scriptures; and families through this means seek to perpetuate their names. They may do this for a season; but if man rightly understood his true position, he would have a brighter object in view. The Scriptures tell us, "that every good and perfect gift comes from God;" that a man can receive nothing but what is given him from above. Men have conquered, and taken, bought and sold, the earth without God. But their possessions will perish with them; they may perpetuate them by law for a season to their descendants, but the Saints of God will finally inherit the earth for ever, in time, and in eternity. Abraham held his possessions on a very different footing from the above. The Lord appeared unto him, and made a covenant with him, and said, "And I will give unto thee, and to thy seed after thee, the land wherein thou art a stranger. All the land of Canaan for an *everlasting possession*." Gen. xvii. 8. This covenant was an eternal one; yet Abraham did not possess the land, for Stephen says, "he gave him none inheritance in it, no, not so much as to set his foot on." Acts vii. 5. And Paul says, "By faith Abraham, when he was called to go out into a place which he should after receive for an inheritance, obeyed; and he went out, not knowing whither he went. By faith he sojourned in the land of promise, as in a strange country, dwelling in tabernacles with Isaac and Jacob, the heirs with him of the same promise; for he looked for a city which hath foundations, whose builder and maker is God." Heb. xi. 8-10. Here, then, we find land given to Abraham by promise, a land that he did not possess; but he will do so, "for he looked for a city which hath foundations, whose builder and maker is God." He looked forward to the redemption of his seed, the establishment of the kingdom of God, and the inheritance of those blessings eternally. If any one doubts this, let them read the xxxi. chapter of Jeremiah, and the xxxvi. to xxxix. chapters of Ezekiel; wherein it is stated that Israel is to be gathered to their own land, that it is to become as the Garden of Eden, and to be no more desolate. Ezekiel speaks of the resurrection of the dead, and the coming together of the bones, flesh, sinews, and skin, of a living army; of the uniting of the nations of Judah, and Israel, in one; and in consequence of the great development of the powers of God, the heathen would be filled with astonishment; and finally, that God's tabernacle should be planted in their midst for evermore. Then let them read from the xlvii. to the last chapter of Ezekiel; and they will find an account, not only of the restoration of the Jews, and ten tribes, but that the land is actually divided to them by inheritance, in their different tribes, according to the promise made thousands of years before to Abraham. In the 13th and 14th verses of the xlvii. chapter, he refers to this, and says, "Thus saith the Lord God, This shall be the border whereby ye shall inherit the land according to the twelve tribes of Israel: Joseph shall have two portions. And ye shall inherit it, one as well as another; concerning the which *I lifted up mine hand to give it unto your fathers*; and this land shall fall unto you for an inheritance." Thus we find that the promise unto Abraham concerning territory will be literally fulfilled. Again, I would refer my readers to the fourteenth chapter of Zechariah. I would then turn their attention to the sealing of the twelve tribes mentioned in the seventh chapter of Revelations, where there are twelve thousand out of every tribe sealed; and then ask, Where are these to reign? The answer is, *on the earth*; together with those who have "washed their robes, and made them white in the blood of the Lamb, out of every nation, and kindred, and people, and tongue." Jesus says, "Abraham saw my day and was glad." What! was he glad to see his people scattered, dispersed, and peeled; Jerusalem trodden under foot, the Jewish nation, temple, and polity destroyed, and his seed cursed upon the face of the earth; or was it the second coming of Jesus, when they would be restored, Satan bound, the promises made to him, and to his seed fulfilled, and misery and sorrow done away; for according to the testimony of Paul, "all Israel shall be saved." Abraham's views concerning land and possessions were not the same as those entertained by men in our day; they were not only temporal, but eternal; and if the world was under the guidance of the same God as Abraham, they would be governed by the same principle; and anything short of this is transient, temporary, short lived, and does not accomplish the purpose of man's creation.

I cannot conclude this subject better than by giving a quotation from P. P. Pratt's "Voice of Warning." "By this time we begin to understand the words of the Saviour, 'Blessed are the meek, for they shall inherit the earth.' And also the song which John heard in heaven, which ended thus: 'We shall reign on the Earth.' Reader, do not be startled: suppose you were to be caught up into heaven, there to stand with the redeemed of every nation, kindred, tongue, and people, and join them in singing, and to your astonishment, all heaven is filled with joy, while they tune the immortal lyre, in joyful anticipation of one day reigning on the earth; a planet now under the dominion of Satan, the abode of wretchedness and misery, from which your glad spirit had taken its flight, and as you supposed, an everlasting farewell. You might perhaps be startled for a moment, and enquire within yourself, Why have I never heard this theme sung among the churches on earth? Well, my friend, the answer would be, because you lived in a day when people did not understand the Scriptures. Abraham would tell you—you should have read the promise of God to him, Gen. xvii. 8, where God not only promised the land of Canaan to his seed for an everlasting possession, but also to him. Then you should have read the testimony of Stephen, Acts vii. 5, by which you would have ascertained that Abraham never had inherited the things promised, but was still expecting to rise from the dead, and be brought into the land of Canaan to inherit them. Yes, says Ezekiel, if you had read the xxxvii.

chapter of my Prophecies, you would have found a positive promise that God would open the graves of the whole house of Israel, who were dead, and gather up their dry bones, and put them together, each to its own proper place, and even clothe them again with flesh, sinews, and skin, and put his spirit in them, and they should live; and then, instead of being caught up to heaven, they should be brought into the land of Canaan, which the Lord gave them, and they should inherit it. But, still astonished, you might turn to Job; and he, surprised to find one unacquainted with so plain a subject, would exclaim, did you never read my xix. chapter, from the 23-27 verses, where I declare, I wish my words were printed in a book, saying, that my Redeemer would stand on the earth in the latter day, and that I should see him in the flesh, for myself, and not another; though worms should destroy this body! Even David, the sweet singer of Israel, would call to your mind his xxxvii. Psalm, where he repeatedly declares that the meek shall inherit the earth for ever, after the wicked are cut off from the face thereof. And last of all, to set the matter for ever at rest, the voice of the Saviour would mildly fall upon your ear in his Sermon on the Mount, declaring emphatically, 'Blessed are the meek, for they shall inherit the earth.' To these things you would answer, I have read these passages, to be sure; but was always taught to believe that they did not mean so, therefore I never understood them until now. Let me go and tell the people what wonders have opened to my view, since my arrival in heaven, merely from having heard one short song. It is true, I have heard much of the glories of heaven described, while on earth, but never once thought of their rejoicing in anticipation of returning to the earth. Says the Saviour, 'They have Moses and the Prophets; if they will not believe them, neither would they believe, although one should rise from the dead.'"[2]

---

[2] Pp. 48-50. Seventh Edition; Liverpool: F. D. Richards. This is an excellent work, and well worthy of any one's perusal.–J. T.

Chapter VI.

Man's Accountability to God.

This is a subject which it may be necessary for us to inquire into, in order that we may find out how far man is responsible. For if man be not a moral agent, he cannot be responsible for the present position of the world; and it would be unjust in God to punish him for acts that were not his, and for circumstances over which he had no control.

By a careful examination of the Scriptures, we shall find that man has had certain powers vested in his hands, which he holds subject to the control and guidance of the Lord; and that if he has acted without the counsel, guidance, or instruction of God, he has gone beyond the limits assigned him by the Lord, and is as much culpable as a minister plenipotentiary of any nation would be who should exceed the limits of his instructions; or a man holding a farm, or vineyard, by a certain lease, if he should disregard the conditions of that lease, and destroy the farm, or vineyard; for the earth is the Lord's, and man was put on it by the Lord. It is not man's possession, only as he holds it from God. Man's body was given him by God, and also his spirit, for the purpose heretofore mentioned. God had his object in view in the creation of the world and of man (which it is not necessary here to investigate); and if man is placed as an agent to act for the Lord, and also for himself, and then should neglect the Lord, he would certainly be held responsible to his Creator. That God had an object in view in regard to the creation of the world, is evident. Or, why was there a consultation in heaven about it? Why the beautiful regulation of sun, moon, and stars? Why the provision made for the redemption of man before he came here? For Christ was "the Lamb slain from before the foundation of the world." Why the arrangement of the resurrection? the New Jerusalem, and the reign of Jesus on the earth? Will any one say that all these things were done, and all nature organized in its present beauty, and order, without a design? It would be preposterous. If God has a design in those things, and man by his wilfulness, wickedness, corruption, and rebellion, should thwart the design of God, and yield himself to another influence, even that of Satan, will he not be held responsible? And whether God has a particular design or not, does not affect the question particularly; for the earth is the Lord's, and man also, and God has a perfect right to dictate what laws he pleases. That the Lord looks upon the world in this manner is evident from the words of our Saviour. "There was a certain householder which planted a vineyard, and hedged it round about, and digged a wine-press in it, and built a tower, and let it out to husbandmen, and went into a far country. And when the time of the fruit drew near, he sent his servants to the husbandmen, that they might receive the fruits of it. And the husbandmen took his servants, and beat one, and killed another, and stoned another. Again, he sent other servants more than the first; and they did unto them likewise. But last of all he sent unto them his son, saying, They will reverence my son. But when the husbandmen saw the son, they said among themselves, This is the heir; come, let us kill him, and let us seize on his inheritance. And they caught him, and cast him out of the vineyard, and slew him. When the Lord, therefore, of the vineyard cometh, what will he do unto those husbandmen? They say unto him, He will miserably destroy those wicked men, and will let out his vineyard unto other husbandmen, which shall render him the fruits in their seasons. Jesus saith unto them, Did ye never read in the Scriptures, The stone which the builders rejected, the same is become the head of the corner: this is the Lord's doing, and it is marvellous in our eyes? Therefore say I unto you, The kingdom of God shall be taken from you, and given to a nation bringing forth the fruits thereof. And whosoever shall fall on this stone shall be broken; but on whomsoever it shall fall, it will grind him to powder." Matt. xxi. 33-44. Here, then, the thing is clearly developed: man's agency; the abuse of that agency; the punishment inflicted for that abuse, together with the awful consequences of resistance to the proper authority. "On whomsoever it shall fall, it shall grind him to powder." God never gave man unlimited control of the affairs of this world; but always speaks of man as being under his guidance, inhabiting his territory, and responsible to him for his acts. The world is His vineyard, and man is the agent. Hence, when God made man, "God blessed him, and God said unto him, Be fruitful and multiply, and replenish the earth, and subdue it: and have dominion over the fish of the sea, and over the fowl of the air, and every living thing that moveth upon the earth." This, then, was man's dominion, *given him by the Lord*. And the word continues: "*And God gave them* every herb bearing seed, and every tree in which is the fruit of a tree." These things were given by God; but to show his power, and his right to be obeyed, and in order to test man, he forbid his eating of a certain tree; and when he did eat of it, and thus broke the commandment of God, he thrust him out of the garden, and decreed that he "should eat his bread by the sweat of his brow."

Again, God demanded worship and sacrifices, and when Cain and Abel offered them, he received one and rejected the other; and further, when Cain was wroth on account of his sacrifice not being accepted, the Lord said to him, "Why art thou wroth? and why is thy countenance fallen? If thou doest well, shalt thou not be accepted? and if thou doest not well, sin lieth at the door." Gen. iv. 5-7. After the destruction of the world, which was in consequence of the people sinning against God, he blessed Noah, and spake to him, and gave him the same dominion which had been given before to Adam; and Noah offered sacrifices to him. The same recognition of the Almighty's power and authority was manifested by Abraham, Moses, the Children of Israel, and the Prophets; by Jesus also, and the primitive Christians. Man was left as a free agent with power to act, and vested with certain powers by his Father, and responsible to him for his acts, as a son, servant, or agent would be to his father, master, or employer. Perhaps it would be more correctly conveyed thus:—a man lets or rents a vineyard or farm, the man occupying it has a certain agency and discretionary power vested in his hands, but always subject to certain conditions imposed by the owner of the property. Hence God made a covenant with Noah, Abraham, the Children of Israel, and the primitive saints. The making of a covenant naturally implies two parties: in such cases, God is one, the people the other. If the people fulfil their covenant, the Lord is bound to fulfil his; but if man transgresses then the Lord is not bound to fulfil his engagement. For instance, in speaking to ancient Israel, he said, "And it shall come to pass if thou shalt hearken diligently unto the voice of the Lord thy God, to observe and to do all the commandments which I command thee this day, that the Lord thy God will set thee on high above all nations of the earth." Deut. xxviii. 1. He then describes what those blessings are; and further states, that if they do not observe his statutes they shall be cursed. The Lord set before them blessings and cursings; blessings if they obeyed, but cursings if they disobeyed. Man, then, acts as a moral agent, to improve upon the blessings which God puts within his power, or not, as he pleases; and it is the abuse of this moral agency, which has filled the world with misery and distress.[3]

Man has lost sight of the object of his creation, and his future destiny; and losing sight of his origin, his relationship to God, and his future destiny, he has fallen into the mazes of ignorance, superstition, and iniquity, and is groping in the dark, and knows not how to conduct himself in this world, or how to prepare for the world to come. For, instead of being governed by the Spirit, Wisdom, and Revelations of God, he is governed by the spirit of the Evil One, "the god of this world, who rules in the hearts of the children of disobedience." They have left God, and submitted themselves to his evil sway, and used that agency which God has given to them, not only in rejecting God, but in obeying Satan; and furthering his designs, which are in opposition to those of God, the happiness of mankind, and the salvation of the world. I know there are many who will ridicule this idea but it is a thing which is plain in the Scriptures. The Apostle Paul says, "The god of this world hath blinded the minds of them which believe not, lest the light of the glorious Gospel of Christ, who is the image of God, should shine unto them." 2 Cor. iv. 4. And if any man thinks he is wise, he has his moral agency and the world before him; and if he can improve the situation of the world without God, he has ample opportunity to display his intelligence.

I would remark, further, that so far from Satan not exercising this power over man, he exercises it to such an extent, and he possesses such an unbounded influence over the human family, that God's purposes relative to man, and the earth, never can be carried out until Satan is bound, and cast into the bottomless pit. John says, "And I saw an angel

---

[3] This part of the subject is fully explained in the remarks on the Government of Man, chap. ii.

come down from heaven, having the key of the bottomless pit, and a great chain in his hand. And he laid hold on the Dragon, that old serpent, which is the Devil, and Satan, and bound him a thousand years, and cast him into the bottomless pit, and shut him up, and set a seal upon him, that he should deceive the nations no more, till the thousand years should be fulfilled." Rev. xx. 1-3. Here, then, he is described as *deceiving the nations*, and his power is curtailed for a season, that he shall not possess it. It is a difficult thing to persuade men that they are deceived; because that very power that deceives them, inflates the mind with self-sufficiency and assurance: but who, that looks abroad in the world, and sees the confusion, distress, and misery that abound, will say that man has acted wisely?

Man, then, is a moral agent, possessing the power to do good or to do evil; if he does well, he fulfils the measure of his creation, and secures his happiness in time and in eternity. If he does not well, and is involved in difficulties and misery, it is his own fault, and he may blame himself. There are many circumstances over which man individually has no control; but I am speaking more particularly of nations and the world, and man's moral agency associated with them: concerning individuals, the Lord will make his own arrangements. The Jews are cursed nationally, on account of their fathers' transgression, and cannot remove that curse, as a nation, until the time come. As individuals they can receive the Gospel as well as others. Their fathers committed grievous national offences against God for some length of time, and finally filled up the measure of their iniquity, in rejecting, and crucifying the Son of God. If they killed the prophets, and stoned those whom God sent, how could he treat with them? He could act no other way consistently than to "destroy those husbandmen, and give the vineyard to others." For if God be the proprietor of the vineyard, and has a right to confer national blessings for obedience, he has also a right to visit them with national curses for disobedience. A nation rejecting God and his ordinances, and killing his prophets, and still professing to be his people, act hypocritically, and impose a great curse upon posterity. And if men will not acknowledge God, how can they expect him to acknowledge and bless them? Again. There are heathen nations enveloped in idolatry; and if millions of people came into the world in those places surrounded with idolatry and superstition, it would be unjust for them to be punished for what they did not know. Hence, if they have no law, they will be judged without law; and God in his own wisdom will regulate their affairs, for it is their misfortune, not their individual offence, that has placed them in their present position. If, however, we could trace their history, we should find, as with the Israelites, so with them. Their present darkness and misery originated in a departure from God; and as their fathers did not desire to retain God in their knowledge, he gave them up to their present darkness, confusion, and wretchedness. See Paul's remarks on this subject, Rom. i. 21-25, 28. For nationally, the conduct of fathers has a great influence over their children, as well as in a family capacity. Hence the Jews will be blessed as a nation, in consequence of the promises made to Abraham, for as I have said before, these are eternal principles; man is an eternal being, and all his actions have a relevancy to eternity. The actions of fathers have a bearing and influence on their children, both as families and nations, in time and in eternity. And those great principles that God has his eye upon in relation to the nations, and to the world, will certainly be accomplished. Hence the stimulus to excite men to tread in the steps of Abraham, that like him they may obtain blessings for themselves and their posterity. And hence the choice of Abraham by the Lord. The Lord said, "I know him that he will command his children and his household after him, and they shall keep the way of the Lord." Gen. xviii. 19. And why did the Lord feel anxious about this? Because of his own purposes in relation to the earth, and because of his parental care of the bodies and spirits of man. For there are matters of great importance associated with these things, as before referred to; and the Lord has felt very anxious, for the perpetuation of correct principles. So strong were his feelings in relation to this matter, that he gave the following law to the children of Israel: "If thy brother, the son of thy mother, or thy son, or thy daughter, or the wife of thy bosom, or thy friend which is as thine own soul, entice thee secretly, saying, Let us go and serve other gods, which thou hast not known, thou, nor thy fathers; namely, of the gods of the people which are round about you, nigh unto thee, or far off from thee; from the one end of the earth even unto the other end of the earth; thou shalt not consent unto him, nor hearken unto him; neither shalt thine eye pity him, neither shalt thou spare, neither shalt thou conceal him; but thou shalt surely kill him; thine hand shall be first upon him, to put him to death, and afterwards the hand of all the people. And thou shalt stone him with stones, that he die, because he hath sought to thrust thee away from the Lord thy God, which brought thee out of the land of Egypt, from the house of bondage." Deut. xiii. 6-10. Here, then, it is stated, that if brother, son, wife, or any one, wish to lead thee from God, thou shalt destroy them; and why? Because in forsaking God, they lose sight of their eternal existence, corrupt themselves, and entail misery on their posterity. Hence it was better to destroy a few individuals, than to entail misery on many. And hence the inhabitants of the old world and of the cities of Sodom and Gomorrah were destroyed, because it was better for them to die, and thus be deprived of their agency, which they abused, than entail so much misery on their posterity, and bring ruin upon millions of unborn persons. And having thus deprived them of their agency to act upon the earth, and punished them for their transgressions, Jesus went "and preached unto the spirits in prison; which sometime were disobedient, when once the long suffering of God waited in the days of Noah, while the ark was a preparing." 1 Peter iii. 19, 20.

It is upon this principle that the world will be punished in the last days for their transgressions, because they have abused their agency, and broken the covenant that God made with them. They have yielded to the influence of Satan, perverted the designs of Jehovah, and brought upon themselves and posterity a curse, misery, and ruin. If any thing further is desired upon this subject, Isaiah has described it plainly, and has shewn the awful effects of an abuse of this moral agency and departure from God, and the breaking of this covenant. To him I refer the reader as a conclusion on this subject. "Behold, the Lord maketh the earth empty, and maketh it waste, and turneth it upside down, and scattereth abroad the inhabitants thereof. And it shall be, as with the people, so with the priest; as with the servant, so with his master; as with the maid, so with her mistress; as with the buyer, so with the seller; as with the lender, so with the borrower; as with the taker of usury, so with the giver of usury to him. The land shall be utterly emptied, and utterly spoiled: for the Lord hath spoken this word. The earth mourneth and fadeth away, the world languisheth and fadeth away, the haughty people of the earth do languish. The earth also is defiled under the inhabitants thereof; because they have transgressed the laws, changed the ordinance, broken the everlasting covenant. Therefore hath the curse devoured the earth, and they that dwell therein are desolate: therefore the inhabitants of the earth are burned, and few men left." xxiv. 1-6.

Chapter VII.

The Lord's Course in the Moral Government of the World.

We will now enquire, What part the Lord has ever taken in the moral government of the world. In the last chapter I shewed that man has a moral agency; acting under the Lord, and is, consequently, responsible to him for his acts, as a moral agent. But does he leave him alone and unassisted to carry out his designs? No. Looking upon man as his son, he has from time to time offered his services and instructions, as a father. He has given revelations, instructing and warning his people. He has given promises to the obedient, and threatened the disobedient. He has instructed kings, rulers, and prophets. He has also protected the righteous, and punished, by judgments, the wicked. He has promised to Abraham and others lands and possessions. He has held out promises of eternal life to the faithful; but has never coerced or forced the human mind. He destroyed the inhabitants of the old world because they had corrupted themselves. He did not govern their minds; they might forget God, "and every thought of their hearts be only evil, and that continually;" but the earth was the Lord's, and he was the Father of our spirits; and although man had an agency to propagate his species, it was given him by God; and if he was so blind as to corrupt himself, and entail misery upon millions of unborn beings, the God of the universe, "the Father of Spirits," had a right to prevent him. And if he was prostituting the use of those faculties given him by God, to the service of Satan, and abusing the liberty which his Creator had so liberally given, although the Lord could not control the free action of his will, he could destroy his body, and thus prevent him from cursing posterity. Hence, if a man transgresses the laws of the land, he is considered a bad member of society, and is punished accordingly; sometimes imprisoned; sometimes banished; and sometimes put to death. Legislators assign as a reason for these things, that such persons are injurious to society; that if crime was not punished, the virtuous and good would be abused; the wicked would triumph; character, life, and property would be insecure; and anarchy, confusion, and desolation would inevitably ensue.

I would here ask, If man acts upon this principle, has not God a right to do so with the affairs of his government? Or should we arrogate to ourselves privileges that we will not allow the Lord to possess? Upon this principle the Devil and his angels were cast out of heaven. The devil having his agency, as well as man, came here, and sought to destroy the works of God; and succeeded so far as to obtain an influence over man's spirit, and bring his body into subjection to his agency; and if man was so ungrateful and corrupt as to yield to his influence, and obey his agency, God had as much right to punish him as he had the Devil; and as he cast the Devil and his angels out of heaven, he also cut man off from the earth, and thus punished the "spirits that were disobedient in the days of Noah." Satan, in heaven, had no power over those spirits; but when they came to earth, he gained an ascendency over them, and not having a body himself, made use of their bodies to corrupt the world, and thus thwart the designs of Jehovah; they must therefore bear the consequences of their disobedience. And if I am asked by a sceptic why God destroyed so many human beings, I answer, this was God's government, they had transgressed his laws, were traitors to him, and he had a right to punish them, as I before stated, to prevent them from bringing ruin upon others, and perpetuating this misery of the human family, in time, and in eternity.

The Lord has given laws, and although he has not forced man to keep them, nor coerced his will, yet he has punished him for disobedience, as a father would a son. A father of a child can teach that child correct principles; but unless he controls or confines the body, he cannot force that child to observe them; he can punish him for disobedience, however, and thus exert a moral or physical influence over him. Our Father does the same. He punished the inhabitants of Sodom and Gomorrah, Babylon, Ninevah, Jerusalem, and many other cities, and will punish the world on the same principle.

Again: he has offered rewards, and given them to the faithful, such as Noah, Abraham, Isaac, and Jacob; he protected the Children of Israel, and blessed them with temporal and national prosperity, when they served him, and punished their enemies; and he would have extended his blessings to the world, if they would have been obedient to him. The Lord has used these influences; but never coerced the will. Hence Jesus said to the Jews, "How often *would I* have gathered you together as a hen gathereth her chickens under her wings, and *ye would* not." God would have benefitted them, but they would not be benefited. Again, the Prophet says, "Because *I have called*, and ye *refused*, I have stretched out my hand, and no man regarded; but ye have set at nought all my counsel, and would none of my reproof: I also will laugh at your calamity; I will mock when your fear cometh." Prov. i. 24-26. These things clearly prove that man is a free, moral agent, and that God never has controlled the human mind, and that, consequently, if man is found in a state of wretchedness, degradation, and ruin, he has himself to blame for it, and not the Lord. The Lord would have given him his counsel if he had sought it; for he *did* instruct men of God formerly, and gave them laws, and ordinances; and he told his people that if they called upon him "in the day of trouble, he would hear them;" and James says, "If any of you lack wisdom, let him ask of God, who giveth to all men liberally, and upbraideth not, and it shall be given him." i. 5. When the Children of Israel served God and obeyed him, they acknowledged his authority, and said, "The Lord is our judge; the Lord is our lawgiver; the Lord is our king; he will save us." Isaiah xxxiii. 22. If the Children of Israel had been obedient, and this principle had extended over the earth, we should have had the Kingdom of God established on the earth, and universal peace and happiness would have prevailed. But man's corruption and degeneracy have destroyed the world, and nothing but the wisdom, power, and blessings of God can restore it.

Chapter VIII.

Whose Right Is It to Govern the World? Who Has Governed It?

Having traced out in the preceding chapters the nature of man, his destiny and parentage, spiritual and temporal; what his object is in being here; what his relation to this earth is; his moral agency; and shown that God has never controlled his actions; we will next enquire a little about the earth; whose right it is to govern it; and who has governed it.

It will not be necessary to say a great deal here about the earth, and its organization, for we have touched on this subject before, and it is one about which there should be no dispute among believers in the Bible. I will briefly state, that Paul says, "For by him were all things created, that are in heaven, and that are in earth, visible and invisible, whether they be thrones, or dominions, or principalities, or powers: all things were created by him and for him." Colos. i. 16. This being the case, without further investigation, we will examine whose right it is to govern it. If the world be the Lord's, he certainly has a right to govern it; for we have already stated that man has no authority, except that which is delegated to him. He possesses a moral power to govern his actions, subject at all times to the law of God; but never is authorized to act independent of God; much less is he authorised to rule on the earth without the call and direction of the Lord; therefore, any rule or dominion over the earth, which is not given by the Lord, is surreptitiously obtained, and never will be sanctioned by him. I am aware that kings and queens are anointed and set apart by their different ministers, according to the different forms and creeds of the several countries over which they reign. There are two things necessary, however, to make their authority legal, and to authorize them to act as God's representatives on the earth. The first is, that they should be called of God; and the second, that the persons by whom they are anointed are duly authorised to anoint them. First, then, it may be necessary to observe, that, if kings and queens are of God's selection, and are his representatives, they must themselves be appointed by him; for if not so, how can they be considered his representatives? The prophet Hosea complains, that "they have set up kings, but not by me; they have made princes, and I knew it not." viii. 4. If they are sent by him, they must understand their office and calling, and the designs of the Lord concerning the people whom they govern, the same as a governor of a province, or a minister plenipotentiary, receives his credentials from the prince or court whom he serves. If, then, we examine the position of kings, and their relationship to their divine Sovereign, we shall find that there are only two ways for this calling to be legal. It must have been given, either by God, through revelation to the ancestors of the reigning kings, and handed down in an unbroken descent to the present time; or, otherwise, given by direct revelation, and they set apart by a prophet of the Lord God. But no nation, kingdom, or king in existence will acknowledge either of these ways. All the kingdoms that are now in existence were founded by the sword, without any respect to God. In relation to their anointing, the question would naturally arise, Who authorised the ministers to anoint those kings and queens?

For if the persons officiating have not the authority thus to anoint, and set them apart, to execute God's law and reign over the nations, their anointing will avail them little: it will be merely the anointing of man without the direction and sanction of God.

Authority to anoint kings and queens, in order that they may be the anointed of the Lord, must be given in one of three ways. It must first, have been given by revelation to the primitive Christian Church, authorising them to administer in this ordinance, and empowering their successors to do it; secondly, by direct revelation; or, otherwise, it must have been transmitted from the ancient Jews, through a lineal descent. In regard to the first, we find no such record in the New Testament; neither Jesus, nor his Apostles, nor any of the seventies, nor elders, ever administered in this ordinance, or spoke of it as being associated with the powers of their ministry. Consequently, no power can come from there.[4]

---

[4] I am aware that the Roman Catholic ministry will tell us, that they have traditionary authority to anoint kings, and to perform many ordinances that are not contained in the Scriptures. Without, however, arguing the point of their authority here, I would briefly remark, that in order for the administration to be legal, it is necessary that the kings themselves be called of God; that this call is requisite, as well as the anointing; and that, if they possessed all the power they claim, they have no more right to anoint a man to be king, who is not called by God, in one of the two mentioned ways, than any officer of state would be authorised to confer an office of trust or honor on any individual, the gift of which was vested in the king alone, if the king had never appointed the individual. All intelligent persons must see that either appointment is illegal, and consequently null and void. The following from a French History, is interesting, and needs no comment: it shows clearly the design of its usage first in France:—
"La cérémonie du sacre était-elle connue en France avant l'inauguration de Pepin?
"R. Non; elle n'avait jamais été employée: mais Pepin se servit de cette cérémonie empruntée des Juifs, inconnue jusqu' alors, pour imprimer à la royaute un caractére plus auguste; cette coutume s'est perpetuée depuis pour tous les Rois de France. Il commença à régner, 752, A.D.
Nouvelle Histoire de France, par Louis Ardent, p. 47. Paris: chez Corbet, Libraire Quai des Augustins.

In regard to the second position, all Christendom deny present revelation; and thus from their own confession they have not obtained their authority from that source; and in regard to the third, if there was authority associated with the Jews to ordain kings, the Christians certainly could not claim a Jewish rite; for the Jewish nation and authority were all destroyed: "they were broken off because of unbelief." Rom. xi. 17, 19, 20. The Christians obtained all their authority to officiate from Jesus Christ, and not from the Jews. Whichever way you look at it, there is no foundation for any such authority, and consequently the anointing is all a farce, for it does not originate with God.

But here let us enquire a little further, Does God set up Christian kings to fight against Christian kings? and Christian subjects to destroy Christian subjects? I know they call upon God; but what to do? In their wars they ask him to destroy one another. This patchwork dominion, and mongrel Christianity, although they may be quite feasible in the dark, yet they present a curious spectacle when brought into the light of Truth.

It may be asked, Has not the Lord given authority to kings to reign? Yes; he has, to two kinds: to one, to accomplish certain purposes that he had in view relative to the nations; to the other, to rule over his people—these were legally called and anointed by him. Of the first kind, was Nebuchadnezzar; he had a kingdom and dominion given to him, so say the Scriptures, but certainly not to govern God's people, for he made, and caused to be worshipped, a large golden Image; and put Shadrach, Meschach, and Abednego into a furnace for not doing so. What, then, was his calling? First, it was to govern a wicked and idolatrous people; and secondly, to fulfil the will of God, in the punishment of his people. As the people over whom he ruled had given themselves up to idolatry, they had an idolatrous king given to them for their ruler, for the Lord, never having given up his right to govern the world, gives the people kings according to their deserts; and although he may not give them *legal authority as His representatives*, yet by his overruling Providence, he places wicked men in a position that they may have power over a wicked nation, both to trouble that nation and themselves. Such was the case with Pharaoh, king of Egypt; and also with Salmanaser, king of Assyria, when he defied the God of Israel. Such was the case with some of the kings of Israel, in the rebellions of that people; and with Belshazzar, king of Babylon, who was eating and drinking with his wives and concubines in the palace at Babylon, when the handwriting was seen on the walls, "God hath numbered thy kingdom, and finished it. Thou art weighed in the balances and art found wanting." Dan. v. 26, 27. Babylon was destroyed; and so fully have the purposes of God been accomplished in relation to that magnificent city, that the place where it then stood is now a desert. And such also will be the case with the nations and kings of the earth, in the last day, as spoken of by Zechariah. "Behold, the day of the Lord cometh...For I will gather all nations against Jerusalem to battle...then shall the Lord go forth and fight against those nations, as when he fought in the day of battle." xiv. 1-3: also read the 39th chapter of Ezekiel. Here, then, is a slaughter the most terrible that could be conceived: the armies actually cover the land, and so dreadful is the slaughter, that they cannot bury the dead, so that their stench shall stop the noses of the passers by. The fowls of the air are commanded also to assemble, that they may eat the flesh of kings, captains, and mighty men; and yet those kings, princes, and rulers will, by the providence of God, be given to the people as a chastisement, that the Lord may punish both kings and people on account of their iniquities. Daniel clearly exemplifies this subject in the following words, in speaking of the judgments that should come upon Nebuchadnezzar. He states, that these judgments were "to the intent that the living may know that the Most High ruleth in the kingdom of men, and giveth it to whomsoever he will, and setteth up over it the basest of men." iv. 17. Another duty that wicked kings have to perform on the earth is, that of being used by the Almighty as a scourge or rod to punish nations that are corrupt. Hence when Israel had sinned against God, and the Lord determined to chastise them, he told them, through his prophets, that he would punish them by Nebuchadnezzar, King of Babylon. Accordingly, Nebuchadnezzar came against Jerusalem, and took the Children of Israel captive to Babylon, with the vessels of silver and gold belonging to the Temple. And God afterwards punished Babylon for its transgressions; Cyrus, king of Persia was raised up by the Lord to chastise it.

But did either of these kings govern God's people? or were they ordained by the Lord? No, only as his sword to execute his judgmentson the nations. Such, also, were Alexander, Cæsar, and others; and hence Paul tells the Christians in his day to submit themselves to kings and rulers. And why? These men were ordained for a certain purpose, and it was not for the Christians to set in order the affairs of God's kingdom, nor to regulate the world. The Lord would do that in his own time and way; it was for them to wait for the time "of the restitution of all things."

Another order of kings were those that were anointed to reign over God's people, the children of Israel. Such was Saul, who was anointed by Samuel; such also were David and Solomon, and many of the kings of Israel. Those kings that were anointed and acknowledged of the Lord were not only kings but priests. Hence, Saul, when he had sinned against God, and the Spirit of the Lord was withdrawn, "enquired of the Lord, and the Lord answered him not, neither by dreams, nor by Urim, nor by prophets." 1 Sam. xxviii. 6. David also acted as a priest, and could obtain knowledge or revelation from God also, for when Saul was rejected, and sought David's life, David called for the ephod, used by the priests: see Exodus xxviii. "And David said to Abiathar the priest, bring hither the ephod. Then said David, O Lord God of Israel, thy servant hath certainly heard that Saul seeketh to come to Keilah to destroy the city for my sake. Will the men of Keilah deliver me up into his hand? Will Saul come down, as thy servant hath heard, O Lord God of Israel? I beseech thee tell thy servant. And the Lord said, He will come down. Then said David, Will the men of Keilah deliver me and my men up into the hand of Saul? And the Lord said, They will deliver thee up." 1 Sam. xxiii. 9-12. Here we find David actually enquiring of God for direction, and obtaining information. The Lord had forsaken Saul, and would not answer him; but he would and did answer David: see also the xxiii. 2; and xxx. 8; and 2 Sam. ii. 1; v. 19-25; xxi. 1; 1 Chron. xiv. 10-14. From the whole of the above we learn, that David took no step without enquiring of the Lord. Solomon also, acted as a priest as well as a king; and it is said of him, that Solomon loved the Lord, walking in the statutes of David his father. And the Lord gave him wisdom, and instructed him in the affairs of his kingdom. When he prayed unto the Lord, and asked of him wisdom, God granted him the desire of his heart, and gave him with wisdom, riches and honor. "And Judah and Israel dwelt in safety, every man under his vine and fig tree, from Dan to Beersheba, all the days of Solomon;" and when he had finished the temple, he offered his sacrifices, and acknowledged the God of Israel; and he prayed for the nation over which he ruled, not by proxy, but himself. "And Solomon stood before the altar of the Lord in the presence of all the congregation of Israel, and spread forth his hands towards heaven;" and then he uttered a prayer for himself, his people, and nation: see 1 Kings viii. 22. And we read that afterwards the Lord appeared to him, and said unto him, "I have heard thy prayer and thy supplication, that thou hast made before me: I have hallowed this house, which thou hast built, to put my name there for ever; and mine eyes and mine heart shall be there perpetually. And if thou wilt walk before me, as David thy father walked, in integrity of heart, and in uprightness, to do according to all that I have commanded thee, and wilt keep my statutes and my judgments : then I will establish the throne of thy kingdom upon Israel for ever, as I promised to David thy father, saying, There shall not fail thee a man upon the throne of Israel. But if ye shall at all turn from following me, ye or your children, and will not keep my commandments and my statutes which I have set before you, but go and serve other gods, and worship them: then will I cut off Israel out of the land which I have given them; and this house, which I have hallowed for my name, will I cast out of my sight; and Israel shall be a proverb and a byword among all people: and at this house, which is high, every one that passeth by it shall be astonished, and shall hiss; and they shall say, Why hath the Lord done thus unto this land, and to this house? And they shall answer, Because they forsook the Lord their God, who brought forth their fathers out of the land of Egypt, and have taken hold upon other gods, and have worshipped them, and served them: therefore hath the Lord brought upon them all this evil." 1 Kings ix. 3-9.

Thus, then, these men, delegated and appointed of God, acted as his representatives on the earth. They received their kingdoms from him. They were anointed by prophets of God, who received the word of the Lord concerning them, as in the case of Saul and David; and if they departed from God, he chastised, or removed them, as in the case of Saul and David, and of which the history of the Kings of Israel is a striking example, and faithful commentary. Those that were faithful among them sought to know the mind of God, and to carry out his designs. The greatest, most powerful, and prosperous rule that ever existed among them, as a nation, was that of Solomon, who asked, and obtained wisdom from God; and that wisdom as a necessary consequence brought honour, happiness, security, riches, magnificence, and power. Thus those kings that were righteous, who received their kingdoms from the Lord, went to war, or proclaimed peace by his directions; they were his representatives on the earth, and governed his people as the Lord's anointed. Yet even the monarchy of the House of Israel was not in strict accordance with the will of God; but originated in the rebellion and pride of the children of Israel, who, wishing to be like the nations around them, being dissatisfied with their judges, desired of the Lord a king. The following are their words, and the Lord's answer: "Then all the elders of Israel gathered themselves together, and came to Samuel unto Ramah, and said unto him, Behold thou art old, and thy sons walk not in thy ways: now make us a king to judge us like all the nations. But the thing displeased Samuel, when they said, Give us a king to judge us. And Samuel prayed unto the Lord. And the Lord said unto Samuel, Hearken unto the voice of the people in all that they say unto thee; for they have not rejected thee, but they have rejected me, that I should not reign over them. According to all the works which they have done since the day that I brought them up out of Egypt even unto this day, wherewith they have forsaken me, and served other gods, so do they also unto thee. Now therefore hearken unto their voice: howbeit yet protest solemnly unto them, and shew them the manner of the king that shall reign over them. And Samuel told all the words of the Lord unto the people that asked of him a king. And he said, this will be the manner of the king that shall reign over you: he will take your sons, and appoint them for himself, for his chariots, and to be his horsemen; and some shall run before his chariots. And he will appoint him captains over thousands, and captains over fifties; and will set them to ear his ground, and to reap his harvest, and to make his instruments of war, and instruments of his chariots. And he will take your daughters to be confectionaries, and to be cooks, and to be bakers. And he will take your fields, and your vineyards, and your oliveyards, even the best of them, and give them to his servants. And he will take the tenth of your seed, and of your vineyards, and give to his officers, and to his servants. And he will take your menservants, and your maidservants, and your goodliest young men, and your asses, and put them to his work. He will take the tenth of your sheep; and ye shall be his servants. And ye shall cry out in that day because of your king which ye shall have chosen you; and the Lord will not hear you in that day. Nevertheless the people refused to obey the voice of Samuel; and they said, Nay; but we will have a king over us; that we also may be like all the nations; and that our king may judge us, and go out before us, and fight our battles. And Samuel heard all the words of the people, and he rehearsed them in the ears of the Lord. And the Lord said to Samuel, Hearken unto their voice, and make them a king. And Samuel said unto the men of Israel, Go ye every man unto his city." 1 Sam. viii. 4-22.

We find that this thing was displeasing to the Lord; they resisted the counsel of God; but as they were the Lord's people, he listened to their requests, and gave according to their desires; he felt bound to fulfil his engagements, and, if they would not walk fully by the rule that he required, to give a government of their own asking, which, if not so good as the one he proposed, was nevertheless sanctioned by him; and that order once established, those kings set apart, and anointed by him, had a perfect right to look to him for his guidance, which they did, and inasmuch as they performed his will, as his representatives, were blessed of him. For kings could not be blamed for the order that existed, they did not originate the government; it was the people, all they could do was to rule according to the direction of the Lord. But this was not a perfect government. The Lord had his eye on something yet more glorious, something in which the salvation, and happiness of the world were concerned; a rule of righteousness, when, not only one nation, but the kingdoms and dominions of the whole earth, should be given to the Son of God; and when all nations, kindreds, people, and tongues should serve and obey him; and as the earth belonged to him, and the people also, that he should govern them. Such will be the case as we shall hereafter show, and a system be introduced that will not only benefit one nation, but that will govern all nations, bless the whole of the human family, and exalt and happify the world. All these things that have existed, are merely temporary arrangements, adapted to the weakness, ignorance, and wickedness of the human family, in the times of darkness, and power of Satan. If the above is the case, in regard to the best of these governments, even that of the House of Israel, what is the situation of those who are governing, without even any pretensions to have received their government and authority from God! It may be asked, What is to be done in this state of things? how are they to be regulated? This is worthy of our attention, but as we shall devote some time to this hereafter, we will content ourselves with saying, this is God's work, and not man's. He has these things in his hands, and he must arrange them; confusion, revolt, rebellion, is not the way to bring these things about; for if the world is already evil, this will only make it worse. Besides, the kings and rulers of the present day are no more responsible than others; they did not make the nations as they are, they found them so; neither are they appointed to govern the world, nor do any of them profess it. According to their most extended calculation, their power would be confined to their own nations. Some of the kings and queens of the earth seem to be actuated by a desire to promote the happiness of the nations with which they are associated, and over which they rule. The Queen of England is almost universally beloved by her subjects, and that deservedly; she has been mild and pacific in her course, and her rule and dominion have been as near right as it is possible for a government to be under existing circumstances.

THE GOVERNMENT OF GOD

If there are evils, she did not originate them, she found them so. She has kept her covenant that she made with the nation, and sought the welfare of her subjects, and they owe her fealty, and ought to render to her obedience. And as she, nor no monarch, is set to build up the kingdom of God, or establish universal rule, as a monarchy without authority from God, it is perhaps as good a form as could exist. The Emperor of Russia, with all his faults of government, nevertheless possesses many good traits; at any rate he seems to reverence the Lord. Some time ago, when the cholera broke out in St. Petersburgh, the inhabitants supposed that their wells had been poisoned; a large number of people assembled for the purpose, as they thought, of finding out, and punishing the aggressors. The excitement was very great. The Emperor, hearing of the tumult, rushed into their midst and said, "My children, you are mistaken in supposing that the wells have been poisoned, and this is the cause of our affliction, this is a judgments that has come from God, let us fall down before him, and ask him to remove his scourge from our midst;" whereupon he fell upon his knees in the midst of the people, and prayed to the Lord to remove the plague from among them. He has a strong impression that God has a work for him to do on the earth; and in this he may be right. Although he is not delegated to establish the kingdom of God, he may nevertheless be appointed as Caesar, Nebuchadnezzar, and others, as a scourge to the nations, and so fulfil his destiny, for as we are on the eve of great events, and a fearful doom awaits the nations, some powerful means must be made use of, in this as well as in other ages, to bring these things about.

Some may remark on the foregoing, Does not Paul say, that "the powers that be, are ordained of God?" Yes, and so say I; but all powers that are ordained of God, do not rule for his glory, nor are they all associated with his government and kingdom. Nebuchadnezzar and Belshazzar were ordained of God, but they were both idolaters. Cyrus was ordained of God; but he was an heathen. God regulates his own affairs; and while the world is in a state of idolatry, apostacy, and rebellion, he, by his providence, overrules the affairs of the nation, as Daniel says, "to the intent that the living may know that the Most High ruleth in the kingdom of men, and giveth it to whomsoever he will, and setteth up over it the basest of men." Dan. iv. 17. But others will say that Paul tells us "to be subject to the powers that be." So say I. God will establish his own government: the cavillings, rebellions, and contentions of men will not do it; and it is proper for well disposed persons to wait the Lord's time, to be peaceable and quiet, and to pray for kings, governors, and authorities. This was what Jeremiah taught the children of Israel to do, "And seek the peace of the city wherein I have caused you to be carried away captives, and pray unto the Lord for it, for in the peace thereof shall you have peace." xxix. 7. It is very evident, from what has been shown, that there is no proper government nor rule upon the face of the earth; that there are no kings who are anointed, or legally appointed of God; and that, however much disposed any of them may feel to benefit the world, it is out of their power, it exceeds the limits of their jurisdiction, it requires a power, spirit, and intelligence, which they do not possess. We see, moreover, that tumults, commotions, rebellions, and resistance are not the way to do it. It requires more wisdom than that which emperors, kings, princes, or the wisest of men possess, to bring out of the wild chaos, the misery, and desolation that have overspread the world, that beautiful order, peace, and happiness portrayed by the prophets as the reign of the kingdom of God.

Chapter IX.

Will Man Always Be Permitted to Usurp Authority Over Men, and Over the Works of God? Will the World Remain For Ever Under a Curse, and God's Designs Be Frustrated?

The above are grave questions, and will necessarily require examination, for they concern the earth and its inhabitants. Their true solution will affect man in time and in eternity. The world cannot remain as it is, for the following reasons:—

First. It would be unreasonable.

Secondly. It would be unjust.

Thirdly. It would be unscriptural.

Fourthly. It would frustrate the designs of God, in regard to the spirits of the righteous; the dead; the progression of the world, and its final exaltation; and also the exaltation of man.

First.—It would be unreasonable for man to continue his usurped authority. If God is interested in the welfare of his creatures, he certainly never would permit, without some just cause, the destruction of his works, and the misery of his creatures; and we have fully demonstrated, that the world is full of abominations, and evils, and that those evils can only be removed by the interposition of the Lord; that the assumed authority of men, and the Devil, can only be checked by a superior power. God holds that power in his hands; he holds the life of the human family in his hands; and the world, notwithstanding its rebellion and iniquity, has to be sustained by him from day to day. Let him but withdraw his governing and controlling power from the earth, and it would wander wildly through space, unblest by the genial influences of the sun, or clash against some other system, involving all creation in ruin: let some slight variation take place in its diurnal motion, and the sea would leave its proper bounds, overflow the earth, and millions of the human family would perish. Let even some slight variation take place in the atmosphere, and the Lord withdraw the sanitory influences that preserve the earth in its present healthy state, and the murky atmosphere would contain contagion, and disease; the pestiferous air would spread desolation, and death; plague and pestilence would fill the earth; and millions of fœtid loathsome beings would be living, and dying examples, of man's impotency and weakness. Even a small insect sent to destroy the grain, accompanied with the blight of the potatoes, such as has already been witnessed, would produce incalculable evil; let these things become more universal, and the death of the human family must ensue. Even so slight a thing as too much, or too little rain would produce uncalculated misery.

When we contemplate man as he is, a poor worm dependent upon God for his daily bread, and upon how many slight contingencies the brittle thread of life is continued, and that the least variation in the economy of God might, in numberless ways, involve the human family in ruin, and then notice his arrogance, pride, conceit, and rebellion; it seems to us mysterious that the mercy of God should be so long extended to him; and we can only account for it upon this principle, that God is too great, wise, powerful, and magnanimous to be moved to anger by the impotent ravings, the empty pride, the little meanness, the swelling pusillanimity, and the utter helplessness, of the erratic, puerile, insignificant creature, man. He lets him wallow in his corruptions, gloat in his misery, and permits him to become a prey to Satan, for a season, that he may feel the greatness of his fall, the extent of his degeneracy, and the utter ruin that his own course, instigated by the powers of the adversary, has brought upon him; that he may afterwards learn to appreciate the mercies of God, see and understand the delusion, and be enabled eternally to appreciate the mercies and government of God, after having first atoned for his own acts and transgressions. For like a wayward and disobedient child, he will be glad to return to his father's house and friendship; and when the vision of his mind shall be opened, which, if not done in this world, will be in the world to come, he will be thoroughly disgusted with himself and his acts, and will be glad on any conditions to find an asylum with his Father.

This state of things, then, is merely permitted for a season, to develop the designs and influences of Satan, and their effects; to develop the weakness of man, and his incompetency to rule and govern himself without God; to manifest the mercy of God, in bearing with man, in the midst of his rebellion; to show man his ingratitude, and the depth of his depravity, in order that he may appreciate more fully the mercy and long-suffering of God, and the purity and holiness that reign in the eternal world. Man has tasted the misery of sin and rebellion, and drunk of the cup of sorrow, in order that he may appreciate more fully the joy and happiness that spring from obedience to God, and his laws. But to think for a moment that man here will always be permitted to subvert the designs of God, and the world be for ever under the dominion of Satan, is the height of folly, and only develops more fully the pride, littleness, and emptiness of man. For notwithstanding man is a weak creature, in comparison to God, yet he has within him the germs of greatness and immortality. God is his Father, and though now wandering in darkness, sunk, degraded, and fallen, he is destined, in the purposes of God, to be great, dignified, and exalted; to occupy a glorious position in the eternal world, and to fulfil the object of his creation. Will this design be frustrated by the powers of darkness, or the influence of wicked and ungodly men? Verily, no. To suppose such a thing, manifests the greatest absurdity, which can only be equalled by the weakness and ignorance from whence it springs. What! God, the author of the universe, and of all created good, suffer his plans to be frustrated by the powers of the Devil? Shall this beautiful world, and all its inhabitants, become a prey to Satan and his influences, and those celestial, pure, principles that exist in the eternal world, be for ever banished? Shall the earth still be defiled under the inhabitants thereof, when God is our Father? Shall iniquity, corruption, and depravity always spread their contaminating influences, and this earth, that ought to have been a paradise, be a desolate miserable wreck? Shall tyranny, oppression, and iniquity for ever rule? Shall the neck of the righteous always be under the feet of the ungodly? No, says every principle of reason, for the Almighty God is its maker. No, echoes the voice of all the prophets, there shall be a restitution of all things. No, say the Scriptures of all truth, "The earth shall become as the Garden of Eden," the wicked shall be rooted out of it; the time shall come when the Saints shall possess the kingdom, and the earth shall become as the garden of the Lord. No, responds the voice of all the dead Saints, we died in the hope of better things, etc. No! say our later revelations—

"The Lord hath brought again Zion;

"The Lord hath redeemed his people, Israel,

"According to the election of grace,

"Which was brought to pass by the faith
"And covenants of their Fathers.
"The Lord hath redeemed his people,
"And Satan is bound, and time is no longer:
"The Lord hath gathered all things in one;
"The Lord hath brought down Zion from above;
"The Lord hath brought up Zion from beneath;
"The Earth hath travailed and brought forth her strength;
"And truth is established in her bowels:
"And the heavens have smiled upon her;
"And she is clothed with the glory of her God;
"For he stands in the midst of his people,
"Glory, and honor, and power, and might,
"Be ascribed to our God, for he is full of mercy,
"Justice, grace, and truth, and peace,
"For ever, and ever. Amen."[5]

It is therefore contrary to every principle of reason and intelligence to suppose such a thing.

Secondly.—It would be unjust: and "shall not the Judge of all the earth do right?" But what right would there be in thus permitting Satan to usurp the dominion for ever? It would be giving in the first place to Satan that which belongs to God. This earth is not Satan's inheritance; it is the Lord Jesus Christ's, he is the rightful owner and proprietor. If Satan be indeed the God of this world, and rules in the hearts of the children of disobedience, he is only an usurper. It is not his rightful dominion, for all things were created by Christ, and for Christ, whether they be principalities, or powers, or thrones, or dominions, all these were created by him, and for him, and he only has a right to rule; but Satan has subverted

---

[5] Doctrine and Covenants, Section 84: 99-102.

the ways of God, deceived the human family, introduced misery, and confusion, and blighted this beautiful creation with his contaminating curse. As an usurper, it would be unjust to permit him to rule; it would be unjust to the government of God, for, if God has a right to rule, no other power can have that right, unless it is delegated, and if delegated, still the right is vested in the power that delegates.

It is therefore derogatory to God, for the world to be yielding obedience to another power. For while God, not the Devil, provides for, feeds, sustains, and beautifies the Universe, and nourishes the millions of people who inhabit the earth, with his beneficent hand and fatherly care;—for him to be neglected and despised, or forgotten, is the height of injustice, and the very climax of perverse ingratitude. But again, it would be unjust to the good and virtuous; this earth is properly the dwelling place, and rightful inheritance of the Saints. Inasmuch as it belongs to Jesus Christ, it also belongs to his servants and followers, for we are told, "The earth is the Lord's and the fulness thereof," and that, when things are in their proper place, "the Saints of the Most High shall take the kingdom, and possess the kingdom, and the greatness of the kingdom under the whole heaven, shall be given to the saints of the Most High." Dan. vii. 18 and 27. It is therefore their righful inheritance, and the usurpation before referred to, while it is unjust to God, is also as unjust to his Saints. Who can contemplate the position of the world, as it has existed, without being struck with this fact, Where has God ever had a people but they have been persecuted? The testimony of God has always been rejected, and his people trodden under foot. Paul tells us that they "were tempted, tried, sawn asunder, that they wandered about in sheep skins, and goat skins, being destitute, afflicted, and tormented." Heb. xi. 37. And to such an extent had this prevailed among the ancient Jews, that Stephen gravely asks the question, "Which of the prophets have not your fathers persecuted?

and they have slain them, which shewed before, of the coming of the Just One, of whom ye have been now the betrayers and murderers." Acts vii. 52. What did they do with Jesus! and what with his followers! We may here ask, Is it right, is it proper, is it just, for this state of things to continue? It is true that the saints have had a hope of joys to come, and this state of trial has been permitted for their ultimate good; but although this is the case, it does not make the thing the more just. "It must needs be," says Jesus, "that offences come, but woe to that man by whom the offence cometh. It were better for him that a millstone were hanged about his neck, and that he were drowned in the depth of the sea," than that he should offend one of those little ones. Matt, xviii. "They that touch you, touch the apple of mine eye." He has cried all along, "Touch not mine anointed, and do my prophets no harm." The saints have suffered and endured, but they have done it in the hopes of a better resurrection; and as they have always looked upon this earth as their inheritance, to deprive them of this, would be to falsify the promises of God unto them, disappoint all their hopes, render inutile their sufferings and fidelity on the earth; and be to them an act, not only of temporary, but also of eternal injustice. For men of God in former days were just as much actuated by the prospect of a reward as a merchant, a warrior, a statesman, or any other person in search of wealth, honor, or fame. The only difference is, the one sought it in this life, the other in the life to come; the one looked for his reward here, the other expected it hereafter; the one had no hope concerning the future, the other had; the one was blinded by the God of this world, and knew not his position, or possessed not a nobility of soul sufficient to make him brook the world, and the scorn of men, in search of a better inheritance; the other understood by revelation his relationship to God, the position of the world, and his high calling, and glorious hope; he sought the nearest way to eternal life, scorned to be captivated by the world's tinsel show, despised the short-lived pleasures offered by the god of this world, and possessed magnanimity of soul sufficient to lead him to acknowledge the God of the Universe, and to brook the scorn of empty fools, and ephemeral philosophers. If persecution's deadly shafts, and superstition's craven hate, were levelled against him, he dared to brook death in all its horrid forms, and live and die an honourable man, a true philosopher, a servant of God, and endure as seeing him who is invisible, in the hopes of a better resurrection. Deprive him of this hope, and you rob the just of his reward, dishonour God, and perpetuate misery and corruption in the world.

Thirdly.—As it would be unjust, so also it would be unscriptural. The Scriptures are full and clear on this subject; they represent Christ as being the rightful heir, and inheritor of this world; they represent him as having come once to atone for the sins of the world; but that he will afterwards come as its ruler, judge, and king; they represent him as the "Lord of the vineyard, the rightful heir" to the earth, and as having hitherto been dispossessed; but they again represent him as coming to claim his rights, to dispossess the usurpers; to take the authority, to rule, and reign, and to possess his own dominions. They represent the earth as labouring under a curse; but speak also of its deliverance therefrom; of its being blighted because of the transgression of man; but that it shall again yield its increase and become as the Garden of Eden. They represent the whole creation as groaning and travailing in pain, but that the creature also shall be delivered. That the Spirit of the Lord shall rest upon all flesh; that the wolf shall lie down with the lamb, the lion eat straw with the ox, and finally, every creature that is in the heavens, on the earth, or under the earth, shall be heard to say, glory and honor, and power, etc. That the law shall go forth from Zion, and the word of the Lord from Jerusalem. That Jerusalem shall become the throne of the Lord, and that the dead saints shall live, and reign with Christ, no longer deprived of their rightful inheritance; but as Jesus said when here, "Blessed are the meek, for they shall inherit the earth."

If, then, the Scriptures are not idle phantoms, if their visions, and prophecies were not mere phantasies, and written to deceive, we have as much right to look for these things as we have to believe in any event that has taken place; but lest any of my readers should be ignorant of the Scriptures relative to these subjects, I will give a few passages which are in themselves as clear and pointed, as any other portion of the word of God.

Concerning Christ being the rightful heir, it is written, "All things were created by him, and for him, and without him was not anything made that is made." He is the "Mighty God, the everlasting Father," &c. "For of him, and from him, and to him are all things." "Thou sayest that I am a king, for this end was I born, etc." "Then the Lord shall be king over all the earth."

The Jews made a great mistake concerning the coming of Christ before; the Gentiles have made as great a mistake in regard to his second coming. The Jews expected him to come as a temporal deliverer alone, and overlooked his sufferings, trials, persecution, and death; the Gentiles having believed in his sufferings, have lost sight of his second coming; the promises of God made to the fathers; the redemption of the earth, and the kingdom of God. Both are wrong; both believed in part; neither in the whole. The Jews, in consequence of their unbelief, were cut off; but when Christ comes again, he will come in the way that their fathers looked for him, as a King, with power, and authority. The Gentiles having fallen into darkness, have lost sight of the great purposes of God, in regard to the redemption of man, and of the world; the restitution of all things, and the coming of Christ to reign. They have so far forgotten themselves, that they are actually fulfilling the prophecy of Peter: "There shall come in the last days scoffers, walking after their own lusts, and saying, Where is the promise of his coming?" 2 iii. 4. But to return: the Scriptures represent Christ as the lord of the vineyard, as the "heir" that was killed; as the "sower of the seed" in the world; as the "destroyer of the wicked husbandmen;" as coming to "rule the nations with a rod of iron," etc.; and to take possession of the kingdom. Daniel says, "I saw in the night visions, and behold, one like the Son of man came with the clouds of heaven, and came to the Ancient of Days, and they brought him near before him. And there was given him dominion, and glory, and a kingdom, that all people, nations, and languages, should serve him; his dominion is an everlasting dominion, which shall not pass away, and his kingdom that which shall not be destroyed." Dan. vii. 13, 14. Zechariah says, "And his feet shall stand in that day upon the Mount of Olives, which is before Jerusalem on the East; and the Mount of Olives shall cleave in the midst thereof toward the east and toward the west, and there shall be a very great valley; and half of the mountain shall remove toward the north, and half of it toward the south. And ye shall flee to the valley of the mountains; for the valley of the mountains shall reach unto Azal; yea, ye shall flee, like as ye fled from before the earthquake in the days of Uzziah, king of Judah: and the Lord my God shall come, and all the saints with thee."… "And the Lord shall be king over all the earth: in that day shall there be one Lord, and his name one." xiv. 4, 5, 9. These and many other things must be fulfilled if the Scriptures be true. These designs of God, which were the hope of the ancient Saints, and of which poets sung, and prophets wrote, were the consolation of all the faithful Saints, Prophets, and Patriarchs,—Jews and Christians. Take these away, and the world, to the Saints, is a miserable blank; the hope of the righteous futile, and the Word of God a farce.

Fourthly.—It would frustrate the designs of God, in regard to the spirits of the righteous, the dead, the progression of the world, and its final exaltation; and also the exaltation of man.

When the Lord created this world, as we have already stated, he had an object in view, not only in regard to the world, and its future destiny, but also as it regards the spirits which were then in existence. Those great and eternal purposes which our heavenly Father, in his consummate wisdom, had in view, when he issued his Divine Mandate, and this world was created, cannot be frustrated unless he cease to be God. And those enlivening hopes which cheered his sons; those spirits that lived with him, when they saw this beautiful orb fashioned, this earth made as the place for their habitation, as their possession, as the place where they should take bodies, where they should live, rule, and reign, not only in time, but in eternity, must not, cannot be destroyed. And yet what avails it all to them, if Satan triumph, the wicked rule, and God's kingdom be not established! They could not "have shouted for joy" at the prospect of this world continuing under the dominion of Satan; at the blight, degradation, misery, and ruin that have overspread it. But if we trace the matter still further, and look at the righteous dead, their position would be any thing but enviable under those circumstances. It was the hopes of the resurrection that made them endure, and it was God that implanted them in their bosoms; but if they are not raised, and if Christ's kingdom is not established, and they do not reign with him, their hopes are vain, their sufferings useless, and the purposes of God are frustrated. In vain did they bear a faithful testimony in opposition to a depraved world; in vain they endured, as seeing him that is invisible; in vain they wandered about in sheep skins, and in goat skins; in vain they looked for a city which hath foundations, as a recompense of reward; and false and deceptive are the testimonies of all the prophets who have testified of the restitution of all things, from the foundation of the world. Take away this, and our highest, and most exalted hopes are blighted; we live like fools, and die like dogs. If the world is always suffered to continue as it is, then is the hope of the righteous vain, the promises of God fail, Satan triumphs, and God's purposes are frustrated.

All the designs of God concerning this world and the work of creation, were perfected in his mind before this world rolled into existence, or "e'er the morning stars sang together for joy." When this world was formed, God intended it as the final dwelling place of those bodies which should inhabit it. And when "the sons of God shouted for joy," it was at the prospect of that exaltation, that they would be capable of obtaining, in consequence of this creation, which they then saw come into existence. And if, as Jesus, they had to descend below all things, in order that they might be raised above all things; still this was the medium, or channel, through which they were to obtain their ultimate exaltation, and glorification. It was by the union of their spirits, which came forth from the Father as the "Father of Spirits," with earthly bodies, that perfect beings were formed, capable of continued increase and eternal exaltation; that the spirit, quick, subtle, refined, lively, animate, energetic, and eternal, might have a body through which to operate, that might be compared to the steam, to an engine; the electric fluid to the telegraphic wire; for, notwithstanding that spirit, steam, or electricity are the powerful, quickening, energetic principles, employed; yet without the engine, the telegraphic wire, or the matter, they would be comparatively useless; these elements might wander in empty space; spend their force at random, or remain dormant, or useless, without those more tangible, material objects, through which to exercise their force. When steam was first applied to practical purposes; when the operation of the magnetic needle, and the mode of communication through the electric telegraph, were discovered; when railroads and steam boats were first invented, something of importance was discovered, and of great value to the human family. The men who made these discoveries and applications are deservedly looked upon at the present time as men of great genius, and as the benefactors of the world; but what was it they did? They did not create the elements, those already existed: steam, magnetism, electricity, iron, coals, water, existed before, and had existed from the beginning of creation. What was it these geniuses discovered? It was simply a method of organizing this matter, the making use of gross inanimate materials to confine the more subtle, refined, elastic, energetic, and powerful, that their combined power and energy might be brought into effect; and that through the union of two powerful agencies, which had lain dormant, their forces might be united, and be brought into active and powerful operation. Thus, then, was the body formed as an agent for the spirit. It was made of grosser materials than the spirit, which proceeded from God, but was necessary as an habitation for it that, it might be clothed with a body, perfect in its organization, beautiful in its structure, symmetrical in its proportions, and in every way fit for an eternal intelligent being; that through it, it might speak, act, enjoy, and develop its power, its intelligence, and perpetuate its species. Hence as the discoveries of those geniuses already referred to, were hailed with pleasure by the inhabitants of the world, on account of the benefits conferred upon men, so when God created this earth, and organized men upon it, "the morning stars sung together for joy;" they looked upon it as God looked upon it, as a work perfect, magnificent, and glorious, through which they saw their way to exaltation, glory, thrones, principalities, powers, dominions, and eternal felicity. They had the intelligence before, but now they saw a way through which to develop it. Through the world's great Architect, their Father, they discovered a plan fraught with intelligence and wisdom, reaching from eternity to eternity, pointing out a means whereby, through obedience to celestial laws, they might obtain the same power that he had. And if, in fallen humanity, they might have to suffer for a while, they saw a way back to God, to eternal exaltations, and to the multiplied, and eternally increasing happiness of innumerable millions of beings. And if, as Jesus, they had to descend below all things, it was that they might be raised above all things, and take their position as sons of God, in the eternal world; that overcoming the world they might sit down with Christ upon his throne, as he overcame and sat down upon the Father's throne. Rev. iii. 21.

But again; this creation is unlike the works of man, which, however excellent, and useful, all bear the marks of humanity, all are more or less imperfect in their structure, and liable to a thousand contingencies, are more or less clumsy, cumbrous, and unwieldy, and must be governed by numerous very limited laws; as for instance, you can convey intelligence, but it must be exactly on the line of the electric wire, you cannot go beyond its limits; you can make an engine work, but it must be stationary; or if moving, must be confined to rails, depth of water, and a thousand other contingencies. None of these things possess intelligence, nor the principles of life within themselves, neither can they impart, nor perpetuate it to others, they are merely machines, to be acted upon by man, and without man they cease to exist; when one is worn out, or broken, another must be made at the same toil and labour; possessing not the principles of life, they cannot impart their likeness; whereas man, beasts, fish, fowl, and all the animate works of God can. Man's works in comparison with God's, are like comparing a child's wooden horse to the beautiful creature God has made, or rather his penny whistle to the music of heaven, or the larger boy's billiards to the motions of the planetary system. They possess no intelligence, no powers, no reflection, no agency. The works of man are merely made to be acted upon; are short lived, temporary, perishable things. Man, however, bears the impress of Jehovah, is made after his image, in his likeness, and possesses the principles of intelligence within himself, and the medium of conveying it to others. He possesses also, power to perpetuate his species, as also to communicate his thoughts, his intelligence, genius, and power to others, that are formed like him. He received his intelligence, his spirit, from God, he is a part of himself,

A spark of Deity

Struck from the fire of his eternal blaze;

he came from God as his son, he bears the impress of Jehovah, even in his fallen degenerate corrupted state. His powerful intellect, his stately genius, his grasping ambition, his soaring, and in many instances, exalted hopes, display, though he be fallen, the mark of greatness; he bears the impress of Deity and shows that he is of divine origin.

Unlike the works of man, the work of God in relation to this earth was destined to be eternal, not subject to be controlled by any little contingences; nor was it dependent upon fluctuation, or change. Man's works might fluctuate, change, or be destroyed, but not so with God's, they were, and are eternal; eternal mind, and eternal matter; organized and created according to the unsearchable intelligence of that eternal unfathomable mind; that fountain of intelligence, forethought, wisdom, and energy, that dwells with God. And this earth, and man in their destination, and all the works of this creation, are as unchangeable as the sun, moon, or stars, and as unalterable as the throne of God. Satan may deceive men, for a season; their minds may be blinded by the god of this world, but God's purposes will be unchanged. Who is Satan? A being powerful, energetic, deceptive, insinuating; and yet necessary to develop the evil, as there are bitters, to make us appreciate the sweet;

darkness, to make us appreciate light; evil and its sorrows, that we may appreciate the good; error that we may be enabled to appreciate truth; misery, in order that we may appreciate happiness. And as there are in the works of creation opposing, mineralogical substances which in chemical processes are necessary to develop certain properties of matter, and produce certain effects; as fire is necessary to purify silver, gold, and the precious metals, so it is necessary to instruct, and prepare man for his ultimate destiny—to test his virtue, develop his folly, exhibit his weakness and prove his incompetency without God to rule himself or the earth; or to make himself happy or exalt himself in time, or in eternity. But again, who is Satan? He is a being of God's own make, under his control, subject to his will, cast out of Heaven for rebellion; and when his services can be dispensed with, an angel will cast him into the bottomless pit. Can he fight against and overcome God? Verily, No! Can he alter the designs of God? Verily, No! Satan may rage; but the Lord can confine him within proper limits. He may instigate rebellion against God, but the Lord can bind him in chains.

Shall the purposes of the Lord be frustrated? Verily, No! The nations of the earth may be drunken, and rush against each other like inebriates; but the Lord's purposes are unchanged. Thrones may be cast down, kingdoms depopulated; and blood, sword, and famine may prevail, yet the Lord lives, and will accomplish his own designs. Man may forget God, but God does not forget man: man may be ignorant of his calling, but not so with God. Man may not reflect upon the designs of God, in relation to this earth, but God must and does; and if in man's madness, his infidelity, his hypocrisy, or his ignorance, he cannot find time here to reflect upon these things, he will find ample leisure hereafter, and the purposes of God will roll on; and perhaps when he shall be preached to, as the rebellious Antediluvians, after receiving the punishment of his deeds, he may know something more of the power, justice, and purposes of God, and be glad to hear the Gospel in prison which he rejected on this earth. But to suppose that the purposes of God will be frustrated in relation to his designs in the formation of this earth, is altogether folly. They will roll on as steadily as the sun or moon in their courses. And as surely as we look in the east for the rising of the sun in the morning to display his gorgeous glory, light up the beauties of creation, and waken sleepy man; so surely will "the sun of righteousness arise with healing in his wings," so surely will the sleeping dead burst from their tombs, and the glorified bodies with their spirits re-unite, so surely will a reign of justice, truth, equity, and happiness—the reign of God, supersede the barbarous oppression, and corrupt governments of this world, so surely will that long night of darkness, ignorance, crime, and error be superseded by the glorious day of righteousness; and so surely will this earth become as the Garden of the Lord, the kingdom and reign of God be established, and the Saints of the Most High take the kingdom and possess it for ever and ever. The time of the restitution of all things will be ushered in; the earth resume its paradisiacal glory, and the dead and the living Saints possess the full fruition of those things for which they lived, and suffered, and died. These are the hopes that the ancient Saints enjoyed; they possessed hopes that bloomed with immortality and eternal life; hopes planted there by the Spirit of God, and conferred by the ministering of Angels, the visions of the Almighty, the opening of the Heavens, and the promises of God. They lived and died in hopes of a better resurrection. How different to the narrow, conceited, grovelling views of would-be philosophers, of sickly religionists, and dreaming philanthropists!

Therefore, as we have said, anything short of this would render inutile the hopes of the Saints; would fail to accomplish the expectation of millions of spirits; and cause

Satan to triumph, and frustrate the designs of God. This earth, after wading through all the corruptions of men, being cursed for his sake, and not permitted to shed forth its full lustre and glory, must yet take its proper place in God's creations; be purified from that corruption under which it has groaned for ages, and become a fit place for redeemed men, angels, and God to dwell upon. The Lord Jesus will come and dispossess the usurper; take possession of his own kingdom; introduce a rule of righteousness; and reign there with his Saints, who, together with him, are the rightful proprietors.

Chapter X.

Will God's Kingdom Be a Literal or a Spiritual Kingdom?

It would be almost unnecessary to answer such a question as the above, were it not for the opinions that are entertained in the world concerning a purely spiritual kingdom, particularly as in a preceding chapter I have clearly pointed out a literal kingdom, rule, and reign. But I have introduced this merely to meet some questions that exist in the minds of many, relative to a spiritual kingdom, arising from certain remarks of our Saviour's, where he says, "My kingdom is not of this world;" and again, the "kingdom of heaven is not meat and drink, but righteousness, and peace, and joy in the Holy Ghost;" and again, "the kingdom of God is within (or among) you."

The kingdom of God, as I have already stated, is the government of God, whether in the heavens, or on the earth. Hence Jesus taught his disciples to pray, "Thy kingdom come, thy will be done on earth, as it is done in heaven." And when the kingdom of God is established on the earth, and prevails universally, then will the will of God be done on earth, and not till then; then will the reign of God exist on the earth, as it now does in heaven. It is this reign we are speaking of, a reign of righteousness. But whenever God's laws are established, or his kingdom is organized, and officers selected, and men yield obedience to the laws of the kingdom of God; to such an extent does God's kingdom prevail. John preached the kingdom of God, or, heaven nigh at hand. Jesus said, the kingdom of heaven is within you. Jesus compared the kingdom of heaven to a husbandman who sowed wheat, and when he went to his field, he found tares also. Matt. xiii. Now what was this field? The field was the world, or in other words, God's rightful possession, where he ought to govern; the good seed are the children of the kingdom, or those who receive and obey the laws of the kingdom of heaven. The tares are the children of the wicked one; or those who rebel against God and his laws. The tares are to be gathered out of his kingdom, and burned; and then are the righteous to shine as the sun in the kingdom of their Father. Again, the kingdom of Heaven is likened unto a treasure that a man found in a field, and sold all his possessions, in order that he might possess himself of that field and treasure; and a pearl of great price, for which a man did likewise; thus Abraham, Noah, Lot, Moses, and many of the Prophets purchased this treasure at the sacrifice of all things. And why? They discovered the pearl, the treasure, and had respect unto the recompense of reward; enduring as seeing him who is invisible. And what was it all for? For the purpose of obtaining present blessings, earthly enjoyments, the pleasures of sense? No! they all died in faith *not having* received the promises; but having seen them afar off; they knew of the treasure, and sold all for it; they "looked for a city which hath foundations, whose builder and maker is God." Wherefore it is said, God is not ashamed to be called their God, for he hath prepared for them a city. They looked for a reign of righteousness—the government of God —they were inspired with the same hope as that of all the Prophets who had prophesied since the world begun, viz., the hope of the restitution of all things. John the Baptist, and Jesus would have introduced the kingdom; but the people would not have it; still, as the apostle John says, to as many as did believe, "to them gave he power to become the Sons of God, even to them that believe on his name." John i. 12. They became sons of God. Yes, say some spiritually, and I say literally too. They made a literal covenant with God to keep his laws; they were administered to literally by officers of the kingdom of God; they believed literally; were baptised literally, and received the gift of the Holy Ghost literally; and became literally the servants or sons of God. But what was their hope? Was it in this world? Yes, but not at the present. They expected the promise of Jesus to be fulfilled to them: "Blessed are the meek, for they shall inherit the earth." And they looked, with Peter, and all the ancient Saints, for a new Heaven and a new Earth, wherein dwelleth righteousness. They looked with Paul, and the Saints to whom he wrote, for a kingdom, not ariel or visionary, but one "which hath foundations, whose builder and maker is God."

The world, as we have before stated, although it belongs to God, has never been under his control. His vineyard has brought forth briars and thorns; tares have been sown in his field; but there has been some wheat, and that wheat represents the children of the kingdom, who have kept his laws and observed his ordinances; and wheresoever the laws of his kingdom have been observed, in the same proportion has his kingdom prevailed. Christ, therefore, organized his kingdom with Apostles, Prophets, Pastors, Teachers, Evangelists, etc.; officers and administrators of his laws, which laws were given by the Lord; they baptized for the remission of sins, laid on hands for the gift of the Holy Ghost, and introduced members into the kingdom of God on earth, and as they were empowered to bind on earth, and in heaven, to seal on earth, and in heaven, these persons, not only became members of the Church here, but also of the kingdom of heaven, and participators in all its blessings here and hereafter. They were now Sons of God; but it did not fully appear yet what they should be, only they should be like him. If he conquered death, so should they; if he overcame, so should they; if he sat down upon his Father's throne, he would give to them that overcame, power to sit down upon his throne, as he overcame and sat down upon his Father's throne. And if Jesus comes to reign on the earth, he will also bring his Saints with him, and they shall live and reign with him. These things are spiritual, but they are literal; they are temporal, but they are also spiritual and eternal. Hence with God all things are temporal; all things are spiritual; and all things are eternal. These are only our phrases to specify certain ideas, which ideas in themselves are very often incorrect: we have bodies and spirits, but it takes both to be a perfect man. We talk about time and eternity,—what is time? A portion of eternity; eternity was, before time was, and will continue to exist when time shall be no more. Spiritual and temporal things are only so, as we form ideas of them. What is our body?—temporal, material? Yes, matter; but the matter of which it is made is eternal, and it will yet be spiritual like unto Christ's glorious body. What is our spirit? —material, spiritual and eternal also? But more subtle and elastic than our corporeal bodies.

Having said so much on this subject, we now come to some of our questions. "The kingdom of Heaven is not meat and drink, but righteousness, and peace, and joy, in the Holy Ghost." What are we to understand by this? that righteousness composes a kingdom? Righteousness is an attribute, a principle, a state of being, not a government; peace and joy are the result of this attribute. God is righteous, and consequently righteousness flows from him. There may be also a righteous man; but we do not say that God is a kingdom, or that a righteous man is a kingdom, but that the kingdom of God is a righteous kingdom. You can say a righteous kingdom, a kingdom of righteousness; but you cannot say righteousness is a kingdom. A kingdom may be governed by righteous laws; its laws may be righteous, its administrators righteous, its people righteous; but to say righteousness is a kingdom, is nonsense. The kingdom of God is a righteous kingdom; it is made up of higher enjoyments than eating and drinking; it is more refined and elevated; it is a kingdom of holiness, virtue, purity; of "righteousness, and peace, and joy in the Holy Ghost,"—principles that exist in part now, as far as the kingdom extends. When the kingdom of God is universal, it will, like the kingdom in the heavens, be all "righteousness, peace, and joy in the Holy Ghost;" yet, it will have its laws, officers, and administrators, and will be a literal, tangible thing. The Spirit of the Lord shall be poured upon all flesh; the will of God will be done on earth as it is in heaven, and the joy and peace which result from righteousness, will be experienced by all the world. What did Jesus mean, then, when he said, "The kingdom of Heaven is within you," or "among you" (marginal reading.) Luke xvii. 20, 21. There certainly must be some mistake here, for Jesus was speaking to Pharisees, whom he had denounced as corrupt men, hypocrites, whited walls, painted sepulchres, etc. Now, who will say they had the kingdom of God within them? The kingdom of God was among them. And it did not come with observation, nor with ostentation or pomp; they might have seen it, but their eyes were blinded, that they could not see; their ears were stopped that they could not hear. Many of us suppose that if we had lived in their day, we should have recognized it among the miracles, signs, and powers that were manifested by him. But Jesus said, "My sheep hear my voice, and know me, and follow me, but others do not." If any man do his will, says Jesus, "he shall know of the doctrine whether it be of God, or whether I speak of myself." John vii. 17. But if they do not, what then? They have eyes, but see not; ears, but hear not. The God of this world blinds their eyes, lest the light of the gospel should shine in upon them. Jesus says, "Except a man be born again; he cannot see the kingdom of God."

And "except he is born of water and the spirit, he cannot enter into it." John iii. 3 and 5. It therefore cometh not with observation; the Scriptures are clear on the point, and show to the last that when God's kingdom shall be more fully established on the earth, the inhabitants of the earth will be as ignorant of it as the Jews were, that Jesus was the Messiah; for the nations of the earth, with their kings, will yet be gathered together against the people of the Lord, to battle, when the Lord himself will go and fight against them, and there will be one of the most terrible slaughters that ever took place on the earth. It cometh *not with observation*. It is a righteous kingdom, and righteous men can see it, and appreciate it, and those only.

I have demonstrated, in a preceding chapter, to which I refer my readers, more fully on this subject, that the kingdom of God would be literally established on the earth; it will not be an ariel phantom, according to some visionaries, but a substantial reality. It will be established, as before said, on a literal earth, and will be composed of literal men, women, and children; of living saints who keep the commandments of God, and of resurrected bodies who shall actually come out of their graves, and live on the earth. The Lord will be king over all the earth, and all mankind literally under his sovereignty, and every nation under the heavens will have to acknowledge his authority, and bow to his sceptre. Those who serve him in righteousness will have communications with God, and with Jesus; will have the ministering of Angels, and will know the past, the present, and the future; and other people, who may not yield full obedience to his laws, nor be fully instructed in his covenants, will, nevertheless, have to yield full obedience to his government. For it will be the reign of God upon the earth, and he will enforce his laws, and command that obedience from the nations of the world which is legitimately his right. Satan will not then be permitted to control its inhabitants, for the Lord

God will be king over all the earth, and the kingdom and greatness of the kingdom under the whole heaven will be given to the saints. This may properly be called the day of reckoning, the time when the world's accounts will be settled; when things that have been going wrong for ages, will be put right; when injustice and misrule will no more be permitted; when the usurper shall be cast out; when the rightful heir shall possess the kingdom; when unrighteousness will be banished, and justice and judgments bear sway; when the wicked shall be rooted out of the earth, and the saints possess it; when God's designs shall be accomplished on the earth, and men resume their proper position. It is the fulfilment of the promises of the Lord to his people, or in scriptural words, "The dispensation of the fulness of times, when God will gather together all things in one." Satan has had his dominion, and has deceived, corrupted, and cursed the human family; but then his dominion will be destroyed, and he will be cast into the bottomless pit; men will no longer be under the influence of his spirit, be decoyed by his wiles, or imposed upon by his deceptions. Religion, and the fear of God, will no longer be painted in dismal colours, or be dressed in the sable drapery of sanctimonious priests, or sacerdotal gloom; nor yet in the forbidding costumes of hermits, monks, and nuns. But, stript of all this religious masquerade, and superstitious mummery, the fear of God, and the observance of his laws, will be looked upon in their proper light. God will be seen, feared, and worshipped as our Father, Friend, and Benefactor; his laws will be kept as being those framed by infinite wisdom, and the most conducive to the happiness of the human family. Virtue, truth, and righteousness, will appear in their native loveliness, beauty, simplicity, glory, and magnificence, for God alone will be exalted in that day.

Chapter XI.

The Establishment of the Kingdom of God Upon the Earth.

How will the kingdom of God be established? We have already shown very clearly, that none of the means which are now used among men are commensurate with the object designed, and that all the combined wisdom of man must, and will fail, in the accomplishment of this object; that the present forms of political and religious rule cannot effect it; that philosophy is quite as impotent; and that as these have all failed for ages, as a natural consequence they must continue to fail. We have portrayed the world broken, corrupted, fallen, degraded and ruined; and shown that nothing but a world's God can put it right.

The question is, what course will God take for the accomplishment of this thing? and as this is a matter that requires more than human reason, and as we are left entirely to Revelation, either past, present, or to come, it is to this only that we can apply. We will enquire, therefore, what the Scriptures say on this subject. It is called the kingdom of God, or the kingdom of heaven. If, therefore, it is the kingdom of heaven, it must receive its *laws, organization,* and *government,* from heaven; for if they were earthly, then would they be like those on the earth. The kingdom of heaven must therefore be the government, and laws of heaven, on the earth. If the government and laws of heaven are known and observed on the earth, they must be communicated, or revealed from the heavens to the earth. These things are plain and evident, if we are to have any kingdom of heaven, for it is very clear, that if it is not God's rule, it cannot be his *government*, and it is as evident that if it is not revealed from heaven it cannot be the *kingdom of heaven*. That such a kingdom will be set up is evident from the following, "And in the days of these kings shall the God of Heaven set up a kingdom, which shall never be destroyed, and the kingdom shall not be left to other people." Dan. ii. 44; and again, "I saw in the night visions, and behold one like the Son of man came with the clouds of Heaven, and came to the Ancient of Days; and they brought him near before him. And there was given him dominion, and glory, and a kingdom that all people, nations, and languages, should serve him; his dominion is an everlasting dominion, which shall not pass away; and his kingdom that which shall not be destroyed." Dan. vii 13, 14. From the above we learn two things: First—that God will set up a kingdom which shall be universal; and, that that kingdom shall not be given into the hands of other people; and secondly—that the Saints of God shall take possession of that kingdom. The Angel which announced to Mary the birth of Jesus said, "He shall be great, and shall be called the Son of the Highest; and the Lord God shall give unto him the throne of his Father David; and he shall reign over the house of Jacob for ever, and of his kingdom there shall be no end." Luke i. 32, 33.

It may not be improper here to notice an opinion that has very generally prevailed throughout the Christian world, that Christ's kingdom was a spiritual kingdom; that it was set up at the time our Saviour was upon the earth; and that Christianity as it now exists, is that kingdom. After what I have already written on the subject of a literal reign and kingdom, this would seem superfluous; but as this opinion is almost universal in the Christian world, my readers must excuse me, if, in this instance, I digress a little. Several writers in the Catholic church, as well as the Rev. David Simpson, M. A., Bishop Burnett, the Rev. John Wesley, and many others among the Protestants, have advocated the above opinion. The substance of their ideas is as follows: that Daniel, by the figure of an image of gold, silver, brass, iron, clay, in chap. ii.—and by the figures of the four beasts, in chap, vii., represented a spiritual kingdom; that this kingdom was set up in the days of the Saviour, and his disciples; that Christianity, as it now exists, is that kingdom, and that it will become universal over all the earth. They state that the four great empires, the Babylonian, Persian, Grecian, and Roman, are represented by the head, breast, belly, and legs of the Image, and by the four Beasts, in chapter vii; and that the kingdom of God was to be set up under the dominion of the fourth, which, as they correctly state, was the Roman. They state, moreover, that the declaration and prophecy of the Angel to Mary, above quoted, were also fulfilled in the first coming of the Messiah; in his preaching, in his gospel, and in the organizing of the church, etc. Many other passages are made to bear the same signification, which it would be foreign from my present purpose to notice. I have referred to the above, as some of the most prominent. Now, with all deference to the gentlemen who have written on this subject (and education, respectability, and talent, entitle their opinions to some respect) I must beg leave to differ from them, and consider, that in trying to support a favorite dogma, they have been led into error; for it seems to me that nothing can be more foreign to the meaning of these scriptures than the above interpretation. Now concerning the four great monarchies being represented as above, I consider it is perfectly correct; but to state that the kingdom was to be set up under the fourth monarchy, or under the dominion of the fourth beast, is stretching the thing too far; and putting a construction upon it which it evidently will not bear. The text reads, "in the days of those kings shall the God of Heaven set up a kingdom." The question is, What kings? I am answered, during the reign of one of the four; and that as Christ came during the reign, and dominion of the Roman empire, it evidently refers to that. But let me again ask a question, Under the reign of what kings was this kingdom to be set up? Under the reign of the fourth? Verily, No. Let Daniel speak for himself. After describing the fourth kingdom, which was the Roman, which is compared to iron, and which in the Image was represented by the legs, he then refers to other kingdoms and powers, as being compared to iron and clay. There were also feet and toes, as well as a *body*, which were compared to powers or kings. This is clearly exemplified in the seventh chapter of Daniel, for after speaking of the four kings, he describes ten horns, of which the ten toes in the Image above referred to, are typical. Those ten horns, he says, are ten kings. It was, then, in the days of those kings, or while those kingdoms should be in existence, that the God of Heaven should set up a kingdom; and not during the power of the fourth kingdom; to which, with any degree of truthfulness, the figure could not apply in either case. But again, it could not apply to the first coming of our Saviour for the following reasons:—

First.—The stone hewn out of the mountain without hands was to smite the Image on the toes; whereas, according to the interpretation of the divines before referred to, the toes were not yet in existence, for they state that this kingdom was set up during the fourth monarchy, which was the Roman, and which is represented in the legs of the Image. Now, as the powers composing the feet and toes were not yet formed, how could the little stone smite that which was not in existence? For it will be observed that after the whole Image was made, the stone was hewn out of the mountains without hands which smote it.

Secondly.—When this kingdom is set up, it is stated "*it shall not be left to other people;*" but we are told in Dan. vii. chap., that after the fourth monarchy which was the time, according to the aforesaid interpretation, for the setting up of the kingdom of God, a certain "horn," or king, should make war with the Saints, and prevail against them; and that "he should think to change times and laws—and that they should be *given into his hand*." Nothing can be more obvious than this; for this power, after the first coming of the Messiah, not only thinks to change times and laws, but "they" are actually "given into his hand," which will not be the case, when the kingdom above referred to is set up.

Thirdly.—When the kingdom of God was to be set up, it was to be "given to the Saints of the Most High;" and all nations, kindreds, people, and tongues, were to obey the Lord, which has not taken place, and never can under the present state of things.

Fourthly.—There is no more similarity between Christianity, as it now exists, with all its superstitions, corruptions, jargons, contentions, divisions, weakness, and imbecility, and this KINGDOM OF GOD, as spoken of in the Scriptures, than there is between light and darkness; and it would no more compare with things to come, than an orange would compare with the earth, or a taper with the glorious luminary of day.

Fifthly.—The kingdom of God, as spoken of by Daniel, was to become universal, which Christianity has not, and cannot, as it now exists.

Sixthly.—The Angel's testimony to Mary has not yet been fulfilled. It is stated, that "The Lord shall give unto him the throne of his father David, and he shall reign over the House of Jacob for ever, and of his kingdom there shall be no end;" whereas he did not sit upon David's throne, nor does he now; he did not reign over the house of Jacob, nor does he now, for the ten tribes are yet outcasts; "the house of Judah is scattered and without a king," and Jesus himself, when asked to divide an inheritance, demanded, "Who made me a ruler or king." He, indeed was a king; "but in his humiliation his judgments was taken away."

From the whole of the above it is very evident that the kingdom, of which these divines speak, was not, and could not be the one referred to by Daniel, or by the angel to Mary; as we have before stated, it was a literal kingdom, and not a spiritual one only. I would further remark here, that a certain power was to "make war with the Saints, and to prevail against them until the Ancient of Days came;" and then, and not till then, was "judgments given to the Saints of the Most High."

We will now return from our digression, and after stating that the kingdom of God is a literal kingdom; that it will be great, powerful, glorious, and universal, and that it will extend from sea to sea, and from the rivers unto the ends of the earth; that all kingdoms will be in subjection to it, and all powers obey it, we will proceed to examine how it will be established. It is compared to a small stone "hewn out of the mountain without hands," and yet the God of Heaven is to set up this kingdom. Isaiah, in his eleventh chapter, to which I refer my readers, in speaking of the establishment of this kingdom, says, "In that day there shall be a root of Jesse, which shall stand for an ensign of the people; to it shall the Gentiles seek, and his rest shall be glorious. And it shall come to pass in that day, that the Lord shall set his hand again the second time to recover the remnant of his people, which shall be left, from Assyria, and from Egypt, and from Pathros, and from Cush, and from Elam, and from Shinar, and from Hamath, and from the islands of the sea. And he shall set up an ensign for the nations, and shall assemble the outcasts of Israel, and gather together the dispersed of Judah from the four corners of the earth." 10-12. From the above it would seem, that an ensign or standard is to be raised to the nations; that the Gentiles shall seek to it; and that the ten tribes return, as well as the Jews to their land; that the dispersed of Judah, and the outcasts of Israel are to return. Now, a standard, or ensign, is a nation's colours, flag, or rallying point; it is one of those appendages to a kingdom that is always respected by its inhabitants. It is used in a variety of ways, and for different purposes; sometimes by the emperor, king, governor, or general, to signify his presence; sometimes by vessels to specify their nation; and sometimes by estates, cities, corporations, or clubs: and always by armies and navies, to represent whom they belong to. If a king had a proclamation to make, and wished to rally his subjects, or try their fidelity, he might send a flag, or standard, and all that rallied to it would be considered his liege subjects.

But here the God of Heaven sets up a standard. The world, as we have before stated, is his; it is his right to possess it. Satan has held the dominion for some time, and the Lord now comes to dispossess him, to take possession of his rightful inheritance, and to rule his own kingdom. In order to do this, he issues his mandate, makes a proclamation, lifts up a standard, and invites all to join it. Those who do may be considered as his servants, as the citizens of his kingdom; those who do not, as being in opposition to him, his government, and laws. As the Father of the human family, as the prince and king, he lifts up an ensign, and calls the world's attention. Now the only rational way for the Lord to accomplish this, is to form a communication with man, and to make him acquainted with his laws. We cannot conceive of him thundering from the heavens and terrifying the inhabitants of the earth, nor yet sending angels with flaming swords to coerce obedience. This would be using physical power to control the mind; but as man is a free agent, he uses other means to act upon his mind, his judgments , and his will; and by the beauty and loveliness of virtue, purity, holiness, and the fear of God, to captivate his feelings, control his judgments , and influence him to render that obedience to God which is justly his due; not until these means fail, will others be exercised.

As the world are ignorant of God and his laws, not having had any communication with him for eighteen hundred years; and as all those great and important events must transpire, and as the Lord says he will "do nothing but what he reveals to his servants the Prophets," it follows, that there must be revelations made from God; and if so, as a necessary consequence, there must be prophets to reveal them to. How did God ever reveal his will, and purposes to Enoch, Noah, Abraham, Moses, the Prophets, Jesus, and his Disciples, and they to the people? God's messengers made known his will, and the people obeyed, or rejected it. If they were punished by floods, fire, plagues, pestilence, dispersions, death, etc., it was in consequence of their disobedience. As God has dealt in former times, so will he in the latter, with this difference, that he will accomplish his purposes in the last days; he will set up his kingdom; he will protect the righteous, *destroy* Satan, and his works, purge the earth from wickedness, and bring in the restitution of all things. The above, while it is the only rational way, is evidently the only just, and scriptural way. Some people talk about the world being burned up, about plagues, pestilence, famine, sword, and ruin, and all these things being instantaneous. Now it would not be just for the Lord to punish the inhabitants of the earth without warning. For if the world are ignorant of God, they cannot altogether be blamed for it; if they are made the dupes of false systems, and false principles, they cannot help it; many of them are doing as well as they can while, as we have before stated, it would be unjust for the world to continue as it is. It would at the same time be as unjust to punish the inhabitants of the world for things that they are ignorant of, or for things over which they have no control. Before the

Lord destroyed the inhabitants of the old world, he sent Enoch and Noah to warn them. Before the Lord destroyed Sodom and Gomorrah, he sent Lot into their midst. Before the Children of Israel were carried captive to Babylon, they were warned of it by the Prophets; and before Jerusalem was destroyed, the inhabitants had the testimony of our Lord, and his Disciples. And so will it be in the last days; and as it is the world that is concerned, the world will have to be warned. We will therefore proceed to examine the scriptural testimony on this subject. John says in the Revelations, "And I saw another angel fly in the midst of Heaven, having the everlasting gospel to preach unto them, that dwell on the earth; and to every nation, and kindred, tongue, and people, saying with a loud voice, Fear God, and give glory to him, for the hour of his judgments is come, and worship him that made heaven and earth, the sea, and the fountains of waters. And there followed another angel, saying, Babylon the great is fallen." xiv. 6-8. Here, then, a light bursts forth from the heavens; a celestial messenger is deputed to convey to men tidings of salvation; the everlasting gospel is again to be proclaimed to the children of men; The proclamation is to be made to "every nation, kindred, people, and tongue." Associated with this, was to be another declaration, "Fear God, and give glory to him, for the hour of his judgments is come." Thus, all were to have a fair warning, and afterwards Babylon falls—not before. From the above it is evident, that the everlasting gospel will be restored, accompanied with a warning to the world. Now, if the everlasting gospel is restored, there must be the same principles, laws, officers, or administrators, and ordinances. If, before, they had Apostles, they will again have them; the same laws and ordinances will be introduced, and the same method for receiving members into the kingdom. They will also have Prophets, Pastors, Teachers, and Evangelists. If they baptised by immersion for the remission of sins, and laid on hands for the gift of the Holy Ghost, they will again do the same things. If the gift of

THE GOVERNMENT OF GOD 117

the Holy Ghost formerly brought things past to the saints' remembrance, led them into all truth, and showed them things to come, it will do the same again, for it is the everlasting gospel. If formerly it caused men to dream dreams, and to see visions, it will do the same again; if to one was given the gift of tongues, to another the gift of healing, to another power to work miracles, to another the gift of wisdom, the same will exist in latter days, for it is the everlasting gospel which is to be restored. If it put men in possession of a knowledge of God, and of his purposes, and brought life and immortality to light in former days, it will do the same again. If it dispelled the clouds of darkness, unveiled the heavens, put men in possession of certainty, and gave them a hope that bloomed with immortality and eternal life, it will do the same again. If it caused men to know the object of their creation, their relationship to God, their position on the earth, and their final exaltation and glory, it will do the same again, for it is the everlasting Gospel. In short, it is the will of God to man, the government of God among men, and a portion of that light, glory and intelligence, which exist with God and angels, communicated to mortals, and obtained through obedience to his laws and ordinances. If the Gospel formerly was to be proclaimed to all nations, so it is now, with this difference associated with it, there is to be a cry, "Fear God, and give glory to him, for the hour of His judgments is come." From this, then, we may expect a proclamation to be made to all people; messengers to go forth to every nation, and the same principles which once existed to be again restored in all their fulness, power, glory, and blessings. The above is the way pointed out in the Scriptures, and is the only just and rational way to deal with rational, intelligent beings; for intelligence must be appealed to by intelligence, and it would be unjust to punish the world indiscriminately, without first appealing to their reason, judgments , and intelligence. But not only will the everlasting Gospel be again restored, and be preached in its fulness as formerly, and go as a messenger to all the world; not only will there be a spiritual kingdom and organization; but there will also be a literal kingdom, a nation, or nations, a Zion, and the people will gather to that. We will here insert a prophecy of David on this subject: "But thou, O Lord, shalt endure for ever; and thy remembrance unto all generations. Thou shalt arise, and have mercy upon Zion: for the time to favor her, yea, the set time, is come. For thy servants take pleasure in her stones, and favor the dust thereof. So the heathen shall fear the name of the Lord, and all the kings of the earth thy glory. When the Lord shall build up Zion, he shall appear in his glory. He will regard the prayer of the destitute, and not despise their prayer. This shall be written for the generation to come: and the people which shall be created shall praise the Lord. For he hath looked down from the height of his sanctuary; from heaven did the Lord behold the earth; to hear the groaning of the prisoner; to loose those that are appointed to death; to declare the name of the Lord in Zion, and his praise in Jerusalem; when the people are gathered together, and the kingdoms to serve the Lord." Psalm cii. 12-22. Here we find, First, that a literal Zion is to be built up; Secondly, that when that Zion is built up, the Lord will come —will appear in his glory; Thirdly, that it is something which concerns the nations of the earth, and the whole world, for there shall the people be gathered together, and the kingdoms to serve the Lord.

It may be proper here to remark, that there will be two places of gathering, or Zions; the one in Jerusalem, the other in another place; the one is a place where the Jews will gather to, and the other a mixed multitude of all nations. Concerning the house of Israel, Jeremiah says, "Therefore, behold, the days come, saith the Lord, that it shall no more be said, The Lord liveth, that brought up the children of Israel out of the land of Egypt; but, the Lord liveth, that brought up the children of Israel from the land of the north, and from all the lands whither he had driven them: and I will bring them again into their land that I gave unto their fathers," xvi. 14, 15. According to this passage, and many others, there will evidently be a great display of the power of God manifested towards the house of Israel in their restitution to their former habitations. Another Scripture says, that "Jerusalem shall be inhabited in her own place, even in Jerusalem." Here I would remark, that there was a Zion formerly in Jerusalem; but there is also another spoken of in the Scriptures. Hence, in the passage which we quoted from the Psalms, the Kingdoms are to be gathered together in Zion, and the people to serve the Lord; and not only the Jews, but the Heathens are to fear the name of the Lord, and all the kings of the earth his glory. The law is to issue from Zion, and the word of the Lord from Jerusalem. Again— "The Lord God that gathereth the outcasts of Israel, says, yet will I gather others unto me besides these." It is very evident from these passages that there are two places of gathering, as well as from many others that might be quoted. For example, Joel, in speaking of the troubles of the last days, says, There shall in the last days be deliverance in Mount Zion, and in Jerusalem. Now, he never could say with propriety in Mount Zion, and in Jerusalem, if these were not two places. The ancient Zion was in Jerusalem. It would not be proper to say in London, and in London; but you could say in London and in Edinburgh, in New York and in Philadelphia, in Frankfort and in Brussels; and so you can say in Zion and in Jerusalem. But again, the Jews are to be gathered to Jerusalem in unbelief, as spoken of in Zechariah; and when the Messiah appears among them, being ignorant of Jesus, they shall ask, "What are these wounds in thy hands?" Then he shall answer, "Those with which I was wounded in the house of my friends." xiii. 6. And then a fountain shall be opened for the house of David, and the inhabitants of Jerusalem, and they will enter into the covenant by baptism, xiii. 1. But the people of Zion the Lord will take them one of a city, and two of a family, and bring them there, and give them pastors after his own heart, that shall feed them with knowledge and understanding. Jer. iii. 14, 15. The people there are to be all righteous. It is the last Zion that we wish more particularly to speak of at present, as associated with the kingdom of God; and, as we are now searching out the manner in which the kingdom of God will be established, it is to us a matter of great importance. There are very great judgments spoken of in the last days, as the consequence of man's departure from God; these we have already referred to in part; but as we have mentioned, the Gospel must again be preached as a warning unto all nations, and accompanied with it is to be a proclamation, "Fear God, and give glory to him, for the hour of his judgments is come." Rev. xiv. 7. But the people would very reasonably be heard to enquire, what can we do? What hope have we? If war comes, we cannot either prevent or avoid it. If plague stalks through the earth, what guarantee have we of deliverance. You say you have come as messengers of mercy to us, and as the messengers of the nations. What shall we do? Let Isaiah answer: he has told the tale of war, and defined the remedy. This shall be the answer of the messenger of the nations, that "the Lord hath founded Zion, and the poor of his people shall trust in it." xiv. 32. Yes, says Joel, when this great and terrible day of the Lord comes, there shall be deliverance in Mount Zion, and in Jerusalem, as the Lord hath said, and in the remnant whom the Lord shall call. ii. 32. Yes, says Jeremiah, He will take them one of a city, and two of a family, and bring them to Zion, and give them pastors after his own heart, that shall feed them with knowledge and understanding, iii. 14, 15. The proclamation to the world will be the means of establishing this Zion, by gathering together multitudes of people from among all nations. For there are multitudes among all nations who are sincerely desirous to do the will of God, when they are made acquainted with it; but having been cajoled with priestcraft and abominations so long, they know not which course to steer, and are jealous of almost everything. As it was formerly, so will it be in the latter times. Jesus said, "My sheep hear my voice, and know me, and follow me, and a stranger they will not follow, for they know not the voice of strangers." Those who love truth, and desire to be governed by it, will embrace it, and enter into the covenant which the Lord will make with his people in the last days, and be gathered with them; they will be taught of the Lord in Zion, will form his kingdom on the earth, and will be prepared for the Lord when he comes to take possession of his kingdom. For "when the Lord shall build up Zion, he shall appear in his glory," and not before. But if Zion is never built up, the Lord never will come, for he must have a people, and a place to come to. The prophets hailed this day with pleasure, as the ushering in of those glorious times, which were to follow. Micah says, "But in the last days it shall come to pass, that the mountain of the house of the Lord shall be established in the top of the mountains, and it shall be exalted above the hills; and people shall flow unto it. And many nations shall come, and say, Come, and let us go up to the mountain of the Lord, and to the house of the God of Jacob; and he will teach us of his ways, and we will walk in his paths; for the law shall go forth of Zion, and the word of the Lord from Jerusalem." iv. 1, 2. Isaiah with rapture gazed upon the scene, and in ecstacy cried out, "Who are these that fly as a cloud, and as the doves to their windows? Surely the isles shall wait for me, and the ships of Tarshish first, to bring thy sons from afar, their silver and their gold with them, unto the name of the Lord thy God, and to the Holy One of Israel, because he hath glorified thee. And the sons of strangers shall build up thy walls, and their kings shall minister unto thee." lx. 8-10. You will find by reading the 14th verse, that this place is to be called "The City of the Lord; the Zion of the Holy One of Israel." Here then we find, that the Lord will have a house built; that it shall be upon the tops of the mountains, and be exalted above the hills; that many nations shall go there, to learn the will of the Lord, and that the law shall go forth from Zion. That the people shall come as clouds to it; that they shall take their silver and gold with them. That God's worship will be known, and the religion of the Lord will lose its forbidding aspect. And God, and his religion, be popular among the nations of the earth.

This brings us to another means that will be made use of, for the establishment of the kingdom of God; for, before this, he will rebuke strong nations that are *afar off. And before they "beat their swords into ploughshares, and their spears into pruning hooks, and nations shall have war no more."*[6] there will be a time of terrible trouble, and distress, of war and calamity, such as never has been before on the earth. Having noticed in the above that a standard will be raised to the nations, that the Gospel will be preached again to all people and a proclamation be made to all nations; that a literal Zion will be built; that the righteous will flock to that Zion, and be taught of the Lord, and be prepared for his coming; that great multitudes will flow to Zion, and the blessing of God dwell there; we now come to point out another way that the kingdom of God will be established, viz., by judgments , that the nations may be purified and prepared for an universal reign.

Before the Lord destroyed the old world, he directed Noah to prepare an ark; before the cities of Sodom and Gomorrah were destroyed, he told Lot to "flee to the mountains;" before Jerusalem was destroyed, Jesus gave his disciples warning, and told them to "flee out of it;" and before the destruction of the world, a message is sent; after this, the nations will be judged, for God is now preparing his own kingdom for his own reign, and will not be thwarted by any conflicting

---

[6] If any one wish further information on this subject, I refer them to O. Pratt's "New Jerusalem."–Liverpool: S. W. Richards.

influence, or opposing power. The testimony of God is first to be made known, the standard is to be raised; the Gospel of the kingdom is to be preached to all nations, the world is to be warned, and then come the troubles. The whole world is in confusion, morally, politically, and religiously; but a voice was to be heard, "Come out of her, my people, that you partake not of her sins, and that ye receive not of her plagues." John saw an angel having the everlasting Gospel to preach to every nation, kindred, people, and tongue. And afterwards there was another cried, "Babylon is fallen." Isaiah, after describing some of the most terrible calamities that should overtake that people, says, "The noise of a multitude in the mountains, like as of a great people; a tumultuous noise of the kingdoms of nations gathered together: the Lord of hosts mustereth the host of the battle .... Pangs shall take hold of them, and they shall be in pain, as a woman that travaileth." That "the day of the Lord cometh, cruel both with wrath and fierce anger, to lay the land desolate, and shall destroy the sinners thereof out of it; for the stars of heaven, and the constellations thereof, shall not give their light: the sun shall be darkened in his going forth; and the moon shall not cause her light to shine. And I will punish the world for their evil, and the wicked for their iniquity, and I will cause the arrogancy of the proud to cease, and will lay low the haughtiness of the terrible. I will make a man more precious than fine gold." xiii. 4-12. After enumerating many other things concerning Babylon and Assyria, as types of things to come, he says, "This is the purpose that is purposed upon the whole earth: and this is the hand that is stretched out upon all the nations." xiv. 26. He says again, "Behold the Lord maketh the earth empty, and maketh it waste, and turneth it upside down, and scattereth abroad the inhabitants thereof. And it shall be, as with the people so with the priest; as with the servant, so with his master.... The land shall be utterly emptied, and utterly spoiled: for the Lord hath spoken this word... The earth also is defiled under the inhabitants thereof, because they have transgressed the laws, changed the ordinance, broken the everlasting covenant." xxiv. 1-5. From the above, it would seem that terrible judgments await the inhabitants of the world; that there will be a general destruction; the world will be full of war, and confusion, the nations of the earth will be convulsed, and the wicked hurled out of it. Jesus said, when on the earth, "For nation shall rise against nation, and kingdom against kingdom; and there shall be famines and pestilences and earthquakes in divers places; men's hearts shall fail them for fear of those things that are coming on the earth." Jesus came first as the babe of Bethlehem; he will come again, "and rule nations with a rod of iron, and dash them in pieces like a potter's vessel." Isaiah says, "There shall come forth a rod out of the stem of Jesse, and a Branch shall grow out of his roots. And the Spirit of the Lord shall rest upon him, the spirit of wisdom and understanding, the spirit of counsel and might, the spirit of knowledge and of the fear of the Lord; and shall make him of quick understanding in the fear of the Lord; and he shall not judge after the sight of his eyes, neither reprove after the hearing of his ears; but with righteousness shall he judge the poor, and reprove with equity for the meek of the earth; and he shall smite the earth with the rod of his mouth, and with the breath of his lips shall he slay the wicked, and righteousness shall be the girdle of his loins, and faithfulness the girdle of his reins." xi. 1-5. The first of this was fulfilled when our Saviour came on this earth before; the second will be when he comes again, "he will smite the earth with the rod of his mouth, and with the breath of his lips will he slay the wicked." The spirit of the Lord will be withdrawn from the nations, and after rejecting the truth, they will be left in darkness, to grope their way, and being full of the spirit of wickedness, they will rage and war against each other, and finally, after dreadful struggles, plagues, pestilence, famine, etc., instigated by the powers of darkness, there will be a great gathering of the nations

THE GOVERNMENT OF GOD

against Jerusalem, for they will be infuriated against its inhabitants, and mighty hosts will assemble, so that they will be like a cloud to cover the land, and the Lord will appear himself to the deliverance of his people and the destruction of the wicked. Zech xiv. Let any one compare this chapter with Ezekiel xxxviii. and xxxix., and he will find one of the most terrible destructions described, that is possible to conceive of; and then turn to the second Psalm, where David describes the kings of the earth taking counsel against the Lord, and against his anointed. He says, He that sitteth in the heavens shall laugh; the Lord shall have them in derision.... That he will set his king upon his holy hill in Zion, that he will give him the heathen for his inheritance, and the uttermost parts of the earth for his possession.... That he will break them with a rod of iron, and dash them in pieces like a potter's vessel; and then he concludes by saying, Be wise, therefore, O ye kings; be instructed, ye judges of the earth, serve the Lord with fear, and rejoice with trembling; kiss the son, lest he be angry, and ye perish from the way, when his wrath is kindled but a little.

In making a brief summary of what we have said before in relation to the means to be employed for the establishment of the Kingdom of God, we find the following:—

1st.—That it will be not only a spiritual kingdom, but a temporal and literal one also.

2nd.—That if it is the Kingdom of Heaven, it must be revealed from the heavens.

3rd.—That a standard is to be lifted up, by the Lord, to the nations.

4th.—That an Angel is to come with the everlasting Gospel, which is to be proclaimed to every nation, kindred, people, and tongue; that it is to be the same as the ancient one, and that the same powers and blessings will attend it.

5th.—That not only will the Ancient Gospel be preached, but there will accompany it a declaration of judgments to the nations.

6th.—That there will be a literal Zion, or gathering of the Saints to Zion, as well as a gathering of the Jews to Jerusalem.

7th.—That when this has taken place, the Spirit of God will be withdrawn from the nations, and they will war with and destroy each other.

8th.—That judgments will also overtake them, from the Lord, plague, pestilence, famine, etc.

9th.—That the nations, having lost the Spirit of God, will assemble to fight against the Lord's people, being full of the spirit of unrighteousness, and opposed to the rule and government of God.

10th.—That when they do, the Lord will come and fight against them himself; overthrow their armies, assert his own right, rule the nations with a rod of iron, root the wicked out of the earth, and take possession of his own kingdom. I might here further state, that when the Lord does come to exercise judgments upon the ungodly, to make an end of sin, and bring in everlasting righteousness, he will establish his own laws, demand universal obedience, and cause wickedness and misrule to cease. He will issue his commands, and they must be obeyed; and if the nations of the earth observe not his laws, "they will have no rain." And they will be taught by more forcible means than moral suasion, that they are dependant upon God; for the Lord will demand obedience, and the Scriptures say, time and again, that the wicked shall be rooted out of the land, and the righteous and the meek shall inherit the earth. The Lord, after trying man's rule for thousands of years, now takes the reins of government into his own hands, and makes use of the only possible means of asserting his rights. For if the wicked never were cut off, the righteous never could rule; and if the Devil was still suffered to bear rule, God could not, at the same time; consequently after long delay, he whose right it is, takes possession of the kingdom; and the kingdom, and the greatness of the kingdom under the whole heavens, shall be given to the Saints of the Most High God; and the world will assume that position for which it was made. A King shall rule in righteousness, and Princes shall decree judgments . The knowledge of the Lord will spread, and extend under the auspices of this government. Guided by his counsels, and under his direction, all those, purposes designed of Him, from the commencement, in relation to both living and dead, will be in a fair way for their accomplishment.

Chapter XII.

The Effects of the Establishment of Christ's Kingdom, or the Reign of God Upon the Earth.

Having said so much pertaining to the Kingdom, we come to our last proposition, and enquire, What will be the effects of the establishment of Christ's kingdom, or the reign of God on the earth?

This is, indeed, a grand and important question, and requires our most serious and calm deliberation. If, after all this distress, tribulation, war, bloodshed, and sacrifice of human life, the condition of the world is no better, man is certainly in a most unhappy, hopeless situation. If it is nothing more than some of the changes contemplated by man, from one species of government to another, and we must still have war, bloodshed, and disorder, and be subject to the caprices of tyrants, or the anarchy of mobs, our prospects are indeed gloomy, and our hopes vain; we may as well "eat and drink, for tomorrow we die;" for, as we have already proven, under the most improved state of human governments we should still be subject to all the ills which flesh is heir to, without any redeeming hope. But this is not a transient, short-lived change; it is something decreed by God in relation to the earth and man, from before the commencement of the world; even the dispossessing of Satan, the destruction of the ungodly, and the reign of God; or in other words, putting the moral world in the same position in which the physical world is—under the direction of the Almighty. It is the doing away with war, bloodshed, misery, disease, and sin, and the ushering in of a kingdom of peace, righteousness, justice, happiness, and prosperity. It is the restoration of the earth and man to their primeval glory, and pristine excellence; in fact, the "restitution of all things spoken of by all the prophets since the world began."

Now, restoration signifies a bringing back, and must refer to something which existed before; for if it did not exist before, it could not be restored. I cannot describe this better than Parley P. Pratt has done in his "Voice of Warning," and shall therefore make the following extract:—

"This is one of the most important subjects upon which the human mind can contemplate; and one perhaps as little understood, in the present age, as any other now lying over the face of prophecy. But however neglected at the present time, it was once the ground-work of the faith, hope, and joy of the Saints. It was a correct understanding of this subject, and firm belief in it, that influenced all their movements. Their minds once fastening upon it, they could not be shaken from their purposes; their faith was firm, their joy constant, and their hope like an anchor to the soul, both sure and stedfast, reaching to that within the veil. It was this that enabled them to rejoice in the midst of tribulation, persecution, sword, and flame; and in view of this, they took joyfully the spoiling of their goods, and gladly wandered as strangers and pilgrims on the earth. For they sought a country, a city, and an inheritance, that none but a Saint ever thought of, understood, or even hoped for.

"Now, we can never understand precisely what is meant by restoration, unless we understand what is lost or taken away;

for instance, when we offer to restore any thing to a man, it is as much as to say he once possessed it, but had lost it, and we propose to replace or put him in possession of that which he once had; therefore, when a prophet speaks of the restoration of all things, he means that all things have undergone a change, and are to be again restored to their primitive order, even as they first existed.

"First, then, it becomes necessary for us to take a view of creation, as it rolled in purity from the hand of its Creator; and if we can discover the true state in which it then existed, and understand the changes that have taken place since, then we shall be able to understand what is to be restored; and thus our minds being prepared, we shall be looking for the very things which will come, and shall be in no danger of lifting our puny arm, in ignorance, to oppose the things of God.

"First, then, we will take a view of the earth, as to its surface, local situation, and productions.

"When God had created the heavens and the earth, and separated the light from the darkness, his next great command was to the waters, Gen. i. 9,—'And God said, let the waters under the heaven be gathered together into *one place*, and let the dry land appear: and it was so.' From this we learn a marvellous fact, which very few have ever realized or believed in this benighted age; we learn that the waters, which are now divided into oceans, seas, and lakes, were then all gathered together, into *one* vast ocean; and, consequently, that the land, which is now torn asunder, and divided into continents and islands, almost innumerable, was then *one* vast continent or body, not separated as it is now.

"Second, we hear the Lord God pronounce the earth, as well as every thing else, very good. From this we learn that there were neither deserts, barren places, stagnant swamps, rough, broken, rugged hills, nor vast mountains covered with eternal snow; and no part of it was located in the frigid zone, so as to render its climate dreary and unproductive, subject to eternal frost, or everlasting chains of ice,—

Where no sweet flowers the dreary landscape cheer,

Nor plenteous harvests crown the passing year;

but the whole earth was probably one vast plain, or interspersed with gently rising hills, and sloping vales, well calculated for cultivation; while its climate was delightfully varied, with the moderate changes of heat and cold, of wet and dry, which only tended to crown the varied year, with the greater variety of productions, all for the good of man, animal, fowl, or creeping thing; while from the flowery plain, or spicy grove, sweet odours were wafted on every breeze; and all the vast creation of animated being breathed nought but health, and peace, and joy.

"Next, we learn from Gen. i. 29, 30,—'And God said, Behold, I have given you every herb bearing seed, which is upon the face of all the earth, and every tree, in which is the fruit of a tree, yielding seed; to you it shall be for meat. And to every beast of the earth, and to every fowl of the air, and to every thing that creepeth upon the earth, wherein there is life, I have given every green herb for meat: and it was so.' From these verses we learn, that the earth yielded neither nauseous weeds nor poisonous plants, nor useless thorns and thistles; indeed, every thing that grew was just calculated for the food of man, beast, fowl, and creeping thing; and their food was all vegetable; flesh and blood were never sacrificed to glut their souls, or gratify their appetites; the beasts of the earth were all in perfect harmony with each other; the lion ate straw like the ox—the wolf dwelt with the lamb—the leopard lay down with the kid—the cow and bear fed together, in the same pasture, while their young ones reposed, in perfect security, under the shade of the same trees; all was peace and harmony, and nothing to hurt nor disturb, in all the holy mountain.

"And to crown the whole, we behold man created in the image of God, and exalted in dignity and power, having dominion over all the vast creation of animated beings, which swarmed through the earth, while, at the same time, he inhabits a beautiful and well-watered garden, in the midst of which stood the tree of life, to which he had free access; while he stood in the presence of his Maker, conversed with him face to face, and gazed upon his glory, without a dimming veil between. O reader, contemplate, for a moment, this beautiful creation, clothed with peace and plenty; the earth teeming, with harmless animals, rejoicing over all the plain; the air swarming with delightful birds, whose never ceasing notes filled the air with varied melody; and all in subjection to their rightful sovereign who rejoiced over them; while, in a delightful garden—the capitol of creation,—man was seated on the throne of his vast empire, swaying his sceptre over all the earth, with undisputed right; while legions of angels encamped round about him, and joined their glad voices, in grateful songs of praise, and shouts of joy; neither a sigh nor groan was heard, throughout the vast expanse; neither was there sorrow, tears, pain, weeping, sickness, nor death; neither contentions, wars, nor bloodshed; but peace crowned the seasons as they rolled, and life, joy, and love, reigned over all his works. But, O! how changed the scene.

"It now becomes my painful duty, to trace some of the important changes, which have taken place, and the causes which have conspired to reduce the earth and its inhabitants to their present state.

"First, man fell from his standing before God, by giving heed to temptation; and this fall affected the whole creation, as well as man, and caused various changes to take place; he was banished from the presence of his Creator, and a veil was drawn between them, and he was driven from the garden of Eden, to till the earth, which was then cursed for man's sake, and should begin to bring forth thorns and thistles: and with the sweat of his face he should earn his bread, and in sorrow eat of it, all the days of his life, and finally return to dust. But as to Eve, her curse was a great multiplicity of sorrow and conception; and between her seed, and the seed of the serpent, there was to be a constant enmity; it should bruise the serpent's head, and the serpent should bruise his heel.

"Now, reader, contemplate the change. This scene, which was so beautiful a little before, had now become the abode of sorrow and toil, of death and mourning: the earth groaning with its production of accursed thorns and thistles; man and beast at enmity; the serpent slily creeping away, fearing lest his head should got the deadly bruise; and man startling amid the thorny path, in fear, lest the serpent's fangs should pierce his heel; while the lamb yields his blood upon the smoking altar. Soon man begins to persecute, hate, and murder his fellow; until at length the earth is filled with violence; all flesh becomes corrupt, the powers of darkness prevail; and it repented Noah that God had made man, and it grieved him at his heart, because the Lord should come out in vengeance, and cleanse the earth by water.

"How far the flood may have contributed, to produce the various changes, as to the division of the earth into broken fragments, islands and continents, mountains and valleys, we have not been informed; the change must have been considerable. But after the flood, in the days of Peleg, the earth was divided.—See Gen. x. 25,—a short history, to be sure, of so great an event; but still it will account for the mighty revolution, which rolled the sea from its own place in the north, and brought it to interpose between different portions of the earth, which were thus parted asunder, and moved into something near their present form; this, together with the earthquakes, revolutions, and commotions which have since taken place, have all contributed to reduce the face of the earth to its present state; while the great curses which have fallen upon different portions, because of the wickedness of men, will account for the stagnant swamps, the sunken lakes, the dead seas, and great deserts.

"Witness, for instance, the denunciations of the prophets upon Babylon, how it was to become perpetual desolations, a den of wild beasts, a dwelling of unclean and hateful birds, a place for owls; and should never be inhabited, but should lie desolate from generation to generation. Witness also the plains of Sodom, filled with towns, cities, and flourishing gardens, well watered: but O, how changed! a vast sea of stagnant water alone marks the place. Witness the land of Palestine; in the days of Solomon it was capable of sustaining millions of people, besides a surplus of wheat, and other productions, which were exchanged with the neighbouring nations; whereas, now it is desolate, and hardly capable of sustaining a few miserable inhabitants. And when I cast mine eyes over our own land, and see the numerous swamps, lakes, and ponds of stagnant waters, together with the vast mountains and innumerable rough places; rocks having been rent, and torn asunder, from centre to circumference; I exclaim, Whence all this?

"When I read the Book of Mormon, it informs me, that while Christ was crucified among the Jews, this whole American continent was shaken to its foundation, that many cities were sunk, and waters came up in their places; that the rocks were all rent in twain; that mountains were thrown up to an exceeding height; and other mountains became vallies: the level roads spoiled; and the whole face of the land changed.—I then exclaim, These things are no longer a mystery; I have now learned to account for the many wonders, which I everywhere behold, throughout our whole country; when I am passing a ledge of rocks, and see they have all been rent and torn asunder, while some huge fragments are found deeply imbedded in the earth, some rods from whence they were torn, I exclaim, with astonishment, These were the groans! the convulsive throes of agonizing nature! while the Son of God suffered upon the cross!

"But men have degenerated, and greatly changed, as well as the earth. The sins, the abominations, and the many evil habits of the latter ages, have added to the miseries, toils, and sufferings of human life. The idleness, extravagance, pride, covetousness, drunkenness, and other abominations, which are characteristics of the latter times, have all combined to sink mankind to the lowest state of wretchedness and degradation; while priestcraft and false doctrines, have greatly tended to lull mankind to sleep, and caused them to rest, infinitely short of the powers and attainments which the ancients did enjoy, and which are alone calculated to exalt the intellectual powers of the human mind, to establish noble and generous sentiments, to enlarge the heart, and to expand the soul to the utmost extent of its capacity. Witness the ancients, conversing with the Great Jehovah, learning lessons from the angels, and receiving instruction by the Holy Ghost, in dreams by night, and visions by day, until at length the veil is taken off, and they permitted to gaze, with wonder and admiration, upon all things past and future; yea, even to soar aloft amid unnumbered worlds; while the vast expanse of eternity stands open before them, and they contemplate the mighty works of the Great I AM, until they know as they are known, and see as they are seen.

"Compare this intelligence, with the low smatterings of education and worldly wisdom, which seem to satisfy the narrow mind of man in our generation; yea, behold the narrow-minded, calculating, trading, overreaching, penurious sycophant, of the nineteenth century, who dreams of nothing here, but how to increase his goods, or take advantage of his neighbour; and whose only religious exercises or duties consist of going to meeting, paying the priest his hire, or praying to his God, without expecting to be heard or answered, supposing that God has been deaf and dumb for many centuries, or altogether stupid and indifferent like himself. And having seen the two contrasted, you will be able to form some idea of the vast elevation from which man has fallen; you will also learn, how infinitely beneath his former glory and dignity, he is now living, and your heart will mourn, and be exceedingly sorrowful, when you contemplate him in his low estate—and then think he is your brother; and you will be ready to exclaim, with wonder and astonishment, O man! how art thou fallen! once thou wast the favourite of Heaven; thy Maker delighted to converse with thee, and angels and the spirits of just men made perfect were thy companions; but now thou art degraded, and brought down on a level with the beasts; yea, far beneath them, for they look with horror and affright at your vain amusements, your sports and your drunkenness, and thus often set an example worthy of your imitation. Well did the apostle Peter say of you, that you know nothing, only what you know naturally as brute beasts, made to be taken and destroyed. And thus you perish, from generation to generation. While all creation groans under its pollution; and sorrow and death, mourning and weeping, fill up the measure of the days of man. But O my soul, dwell no longer on this awful scene: let it suffice, to have discovered in some degree, what is lost. Let us turn our attention to what the Prophets have said should be restored.

"The Apostle Peter, while preaching to the Jews, says, 'And he shall send Jesus Christ, which before was preached unto you, whom the heavens must receive, until the times of restitution (restoration) of all things which God hath spoken, by the mouth of all the holy prophets, since the world began.' It appears from the above, that all the holy prophets from Adam, and those that follow after, have had their eyes upon a certain time, when all things should be restored to their primitive beauty and excellence. We also learn, that the time of restitution was to be at or near the time of Christ's second coming; for the heavens are to receive him, until the times of restitution, and then the Father shall send him again to the earth.

"We will now proceed to notice Isaiah xl. 1-5. 'Comfort ye, comfort ye my people, saith your God. Speak ye comfortably to Jerusalem, and cry unto her, that her warfare is accomplished, that her iniquity is pardoned: for she hath received of the Lord's hand, double for all her sins. The voice of him that crieth in the wilderness, Prepare ye the way of the Lord, make straight in the desert a highway for our God. Every valley shall be exalted, and every mountain and hill shall be made low: and the crooked shall be made straight, and the rough places plain: and the glory of the Lord shall be revealed, and all flesh shall see it together: for the mouth of the Lord hath spoken it.'

"From these verses we learn, first, that the voice of one shall be heard in the wilderness, to prepare the way of the Lord, just at the time when Jerusalem has been trodden down of the Gentiles long enough to have received, at the Lord's hand, double for all her sins, yea, when the warfare of Jerusalem is accomplished, and her iniquities pardoned; then shall this proclamation be made as it was before by John, yea, a second proclamation, to prepare the way of the Lord, for his second coming; and about that time every valley shall be exalted, and every mountain and hill shall be made low, and the crooked shall be made straight, and rough places plain, and then the glory of the Lord shall be revealed, and all flesh shall see it together, for the mouth of the Lord hath spoken it.

"Thus you see, every mountain being laid low, and every valley exalted, and the rough places being made plain, and the crooked places straight, that these mighty revolutions will begin to restore the face of the earth to its former beauty. But all this done, we have not yet gone through our restoration; there are many more great things to be done, in order to restore all things.

"Our next is Isaiah 35th chapter, where we again read of the Lord's second coming, and of the mighty works which attend it. The barren desert should abound with pools and springs of living water, and should produce grass, with flowers blooming and blossoming as the rose, and that, too, about the time of the coming of their God, with vengeance and recompense, which must allude to his second coming; and Israel is to come at the same time to Zion, with songs of everlasting joy, and sorrow and sighing shall flee away. Here, then, we have the curse taken off from the deserts, and they become a fruitful, well-watered country.

"We will now inquire whether the islands return again to the continents, from which they were once separated. For this subject we refer you to Revelation vi. 14,—'And every mountain and island were moved out of their places.' From this we learn that they moved somewhere; and as it is the time of restoring what had been lost, they accordingly return and join themselves to the land whence they came.

"Our next is Isaiah xiii. 13, 14, where 'The earth shall move out of her place, and be like a chased roe which no man taketh up. Also, Isaiah lxii. 4, 'Thou shalt no more be termed forsaken; neither shall thy land any more be termed desolate; but thou shalt be called Hephzibah, and thy land Beulah: for the Lord delighteth in thee, and thy land shall be married.'

"In the first instance, we have the earth on a move like a chased roe; and in the second place, we have it married. And from the whole, and various Scriptures, we learn, that the continents and islands shall be united in one, as they were on the morn of creation, and the sea shall retire and assemble in its own place, where it was before; and all these scenes shall take place during the mighty convulsion of nature, about the time of the coming of the Lord.

"Behold! the Mount of Olives rend in twain;

While on its top he sets his feet again,

The islands at his word, obedient, flee;

While to the north, he rolls the mighty sea;

Restores the earth in one, as at the first,

With all its blessings, and removes the curse.

"Having restored the earth to the same glorious state in which it first existed; levelling the mountains, exalting the valleys, smoothing the rough places, making the deserts fruitful, and bringing all the continents and islands together, causing the curse to be taken off, that it shall no longer produce noxious weeds, and thorns, and thistles; the next thing is to regulate and restore the brute creation to their former state of peace and glory, causing all enmity to cease from off the earth. But this will never be done until there is a general destruction poured out upon man, which will entirely cleanse the earth, and sweep all wickedness from its face. This will be done by the rod of his mouth, and by the breath of his lips; or, in other words, by fire as universal as the flood. Isaiah xi. 4, 6-9, 'But with righteousness shall he judge the poor, and reprove with equity for the meek of the earth: and he shall smite the earth with the rod of his mouth, and with the breath of his lips shall he slay the wicked. The wolf also shall dwell with the lamb, and the leopard shall lie down with the kid; and the calf, and the young lion, and the fatling together; and a little child shall lead them. And the cow and the bear shall feed; their young ones shall lie down together; and the lion shall eat straw like the ox. And the sucking child shall play on the hole of the asp, and the weaned child shall put his hand on the cockatrice's den. They shall not hurt nor destroy in all my holy mountain: for the earth shall be full of the knowledge of the Lord, as the waters cover the sea.'

"Thus, having cleansed the earth, and glorified it with the knowledge of God, as the waters cover the sea, and having poured out his Spirit upon all flesh, both man and beast becoming perfectly harmless, as they were in the beginning, and feeding on vegetable food only, while nothing is left to hurt or destroy in all the vast creation, the prophets then proceed to give us many glorious descriptions of the enjoyments of its inhabitants. 'They shall build houses and inhabit them; they shall plant vineyards, and drink the wine of them; they shall plant gardens and eat the fruit of them; they shall not build and another inhabit; they shall not plant and another eat; for as the days of a tree are the days of my people, and mine elect shall long enjoy the work of their hands. They shall not labour in vain, nor bring forth in trouble; for they are the seed of the blessed of the Lord, and their offspring with them; and it shall come to pass, that before they call I will answer, and while they are yet speaking I will hear.' In this happy state of existence it seems that all people will live to the full age of a tree, and this too without pain or sorrow, and whatsoever they ask will be immediately answered, and even all their wants will be anticipated. Of course, then, none of them will sleep in the dust, for they will prefer to be translated; that is, changed in the twinkling of an eye, from mortal to immortal; after which they will continue to reign with Jesus on the earth." Pp. 110-122.

A great council will then be held to adjust the affairs of the world, from the commencement, over which Father Adam will preside as head and representative of the human family. There have been, in different ages of the world, communications opened between the heavens and the earth. Those powers have been separated, and have acted in different spheres, until the present. The kingdom of God on the earth has been small, weak, unpopular, trampled under foot of men, and none but men of noble minds, firm hopes, and daring resolution, have advocated its principles. These men, being possessed of intelligence from the heavens by the ministering of angels, the communications of the spirits of the just, and the manifestation of eternal things, knew of the approaching day of glory, the reign of God on the earth; they understood their destiny, and lived, and died, in the hopes of inheriting these things. Those communications from the heavens developd the purposes of God to them; and in all their moves, they were regulated by the prospect of the future. In the Mosaic Dispensation they had to make earthly things according to the pattern of heavenly. Hence it was said to Moses, "See that thou make all things according to the pattern shewn thee in the Mount." The ark was made, therefore, after a heavenly pattern, and so was the Temple of Jerusalem. Jerusalem was a figure of the heavenly. The sacrifices of the Aaronic Priesthood referred to the expiation of Christ, who appears as the earthly High Priest of the Jews, and as our eternal High Priest and Intercessor in the heavens. His Priesthood was an eternal one, and is after the order of Melchisedek, and Melchisedek's was after his order, and they both were after the order that exists in the heavens. This priesthood with the Gospel, brought life and immortality to light, put men in possession of certainty, and unveiled the future; they knew the divine laws and ordinances, and acted with a reference to them; and being commissioned of God, they had power to bind and loose, etc.

Then they will assemble to regulate all these affairs, and all that held keys of authority to administer, will then represent their earthly course. And, as this authority has been handed down from one to another in different ages, and in different dispensations, a full reckoning will have to be made by all. All who have held keys of Priesthood, will then have to give an account to those from whom they received them. Those that were in the heavens, have been assisting those that were upon the earth; but then, they will unite together in a general council to give an account of their stewardships, and as in the various ages men have received their power to administer, from those who had previously held the keys thereof, there will be a general account. Those, under the authorities of the Church of Jesus Christ of Latter-day Saints, have to give an account of their transactions to those who direct them in the Priesthood; hence the Elders give an account to Presidents of Conferences; and Presidents of Conferences to Presidents of Nations. Those Presidents and the Seventies give an account to the Twelve Apostles; the Twelve to the First Presidency; and they to Joseph, from whom they, and the Twelve, received their Priesthood. This will include the arrangements of the last dispensation. Joseph delivers his authority to Peter, who held the keys before him, and delivered them to him; and Peter to Moses and Elias, who endued him with this authority on the Mount; and they to those from whom they received them. And thus the world's affairs will be regulated and put right, the restitution of all things be accomplished, and the Kingdom of God be ushered in. The earth will be delivered from under the curse, resume its paradisiacal glory, and all things pertaining to its restoration be fulfilled.

Not only will the earth be restored, but also man; and those promises which, long ago, were the hope of the saints, will be realised. The faithful servants of God who have lived in every age, will then come forth and experience the full fruition of that joy, for which they lived, and hoped, and suffered, and died. The tombs will deliver up their captives, and re-united with the spirits which once animated, vivified, cheered, and sustained them while in this vale of tears, these bodies will be like unto Christ's glorious body. They will then rejoice in that resurrection for which they lived, while they sojourned below. Adam, Seth, Enoch, and the faithful who lived before the flood, will possess their proper inheritance. Noah and Melchisedek will stand in their proper places. Abraham, with Isaac and Jacob, heirs with him of the same promise, will come forward at the head of innumerable multitudes, and possess that land which God gave unto them for an everlasting inheritance. The faithful, on the continent of America, will also stand in their proper place; but, as this will be the time of the restitution of all things, and all things will not be fully restored at once; there will be a distinction between the resurrected bodies, and those that have not been resurrected; and as the Scriptures say that flesh and blood cannot inherit the kingdom of God, neither doth corruption inherit incorruption; and although the world will enjoy just laws—an equitable administration, and universal peace and happiness prevail as the result of this righteousness; yet, there will be a peculiar habitation for the resurrected bodies. This habitation may be compared to Paradise, from whence man, in the beginning, was driven.

When Adam was driven from the Garden, an angel was placed with a flaming sword to guard the way of the tree of life, lest man should eat of it, and become immortal in his degenerate state, and thus be incapable of obtaining that exaltation, which he would be capable of enjoying through the redemption of Jesus Christ, and the power of the resurrection, with his renewed and glorified body. Having tasted of the nature of the fall, and having grappled with sin and misery, knowing like the gods both good and evil, having like Jesus overcome the evil, and through the power of the atonement, having conquered death, hell, and the grave, he regains that Paradise, from which he was banished, not in the capacity of ignorant man, unacquinted with evil, but like unto a god. He can now stretch forth, and partake of the tree of life, and eat of its fruits, and live and flourish eternally in possession of that immortality which Jesus long ago promised to the faithful:

"To him that overcomes, will I grant to sit with me in my throne; and eat of the tree of life which is in the midst of the Paradise of God."

Made in the USA
Columbia, SC
17 March 2025